ELVIS COSTELLO
A Completely False Biography Based on Rumor, Innuendo and Lies

Krista Reese

PROTEUS PUBLISHING
London and New York

United Kingdom
PROTEUS (PUBLISHING) LIMITED
Bremar House, Sale Place, London W2 1PT

United States
PROTEUS PUBLISHING CO., INC.
distributed by:
THE SCRIBNER BOOK COMPANIES, INC.
597 Fifth Avenue, New York, N.Y. 10017

ISBN 0 906071 62 3

First published in U.K. 1981
First published in U.S. 1981

Printed in the United States of America
Design and production by Celie Fitzgerald

Photograph Credits:
Black and white (numbers refer to book page): 6/25 (C) Barry Plummer; 8/10/11/12/
13/14/17/19/21/26/93/94/98/103/118 (C) Peter Mavromates; 9/47/53/62/63/
72/89/92/111/114/117 (C) Proteus Publishing; 22/24/38/42/108 Gus Stewart;
31/50 Paul Cox, (C) London Features International Ltd.; 32 Paul Windnam; 35/37
courtesy Stiff Records; 36 source unknown; 41 Max Browne; 44 Paul Canty, (C) London
Features International Ltd.; 48/49 Pan Dickson; 55 Denis O'Regan; 57 Rock Shots Ltd.;
61 Adrian Boot, (C) London Features International Ltd.; 68 (C) 1978 Chester Simpson;
75 (C) Dave Siviour; 77 Mark Gaynor; 79 (C) Paul Edmond; 82 Chalkie Davies; 86
David Muscroft, White's News Agency; 97 Peter Kerkick; 104 Syndication International,
London.

Color (numbers refer to order of appearance in color section): 1/6 (C) Peter
Mavromates; 2/3 (C) Proteus Publishing; 4/5 (C) Rex Features Ltd., London.

Table of Contents

Riviera
GLOBAL RECORD PRODUCTIONS LIMITED

27th March 1981

Dear Krista

I am replying to you partly as a measure of courtesy.

I would like to notify you that I will do everything in my power to prevent you from writing a book about Elvis Costello.

I would point out, in the few interviews Elvis has given, the copyright rests with the publisher of those interviews (i.e. IPC Magazines etc.) If you plunder from these articles you will be infringing their copyright, and I shall vigorously assist the publishers of these articles in nailing you and your publishing company to the wall.

Thank you for enclosing your address. If this matter goes any further I shall pop in for a visit when I am next in New York.

Kind regards

JAKE RIVIERA

Jake Riviera

Executive Suite 6 Horn Lane Acton London W3 9NJ
Telephone 01 993 1481 Accounts 01 993 4734 Telex 894666
Director: Jake Riviera Secretary: J F Jakeman
Registered Office: 65 Duke Street London. W1M 5DH Registered in England No 1332655
VAT Registration No 235 2568 63

My Aim Is True

Even in the daytime, Fourteenth Street in New York City seems to have a tawdry glow, as if the nighttime neon effect never wears off. The street is often lumped in a group that townies warn tourists about, including Eighth Avenue, Forty-second Street ("Watch your wallet"), and Union Square Park ("Unsafe at any hour"). In fact, Union Square Park joins Fourteenth Street, making it a double threat for tourists preoccupied with the strip-show billboards, doe-eyed ingenues wandering around looking lost or enthralled, or any group of whites who look susceptible to taunts.

In the park clusters of young men and boys lounge around graffiti-scrawled edifices. They seem to be muttering to themselves, until you go near enough to make out the words, "marijuana, cocaine, hash, mescaline..." or "loose joints, loose joints." It's business as usual.

Fourteenth is an eclectic collection of merchants, but they all seem throwbacks to another time. Among the peep shows, furniture marts, Woolworth's, and junk shops, down from the coffee shop called the Disco Donut, stands Luchow's, one of the city's oldest restaurants, known for its oom-pah bands and piggishly large portions, where Mayor Ed Koch took the ex-hostages for "Christmas" dinner.

Just two doors east of Luchow's is the Palladium, a huge old theater dating back to vaudeville. Since the mid-seventies, the theater has been

a regular stopover for new bands coming up from the CBGB-Mudd Club circuit or coming over from England's pub-rock rounds. Above the marquee looms a huge mural, invisible at night, showing a goddess peeping around a curtain at a massive audience of wild teens at a concert. According to *Billboard,* 1980's second largest gross at an auditorium was at the Palladium, when Elton John brought in nearly $400,000. And because it stands on Fourteenth Street, where Elvis Costello, the hottest show to appear in months, will play, the carnival market-madness atmosphere will heighten. Just because Elvis doesn't cater to the moguls and avoids publicity, and just because this is American profiteering at its worst doesn't mean the setting is incon-

Above: The Palladium. New York City. February 1981. Right: Souvenir mug from '81 tour. What, no spoon?

gruous. Quite the contrary: There is something very fitting about the combination of cheesy Fourteenth Street and "the man who would be king."

By seven o'clock on Monday, the last night of the Palladium show, the hawking on Fourteenth has intensified and taken on a different character. The bins of crockpots marked "as is" have given way to vendors' trays catering directly to the clientele. They are full of color Xerox buttons, illegally silk-screened T-shirts, and posters. A pin featuring two plastic bubbles whose black frames trap two tiny beads that roll like looney-toon eyes (Elvis's famed glasses) are a particularly popular item. The young men and boys from Union Square Park have moved to stations in corners and in doorways, lounging, dancing to the music from a huge Sony carried by a strap, venturing down the street mumbling "Selling tickets, selling tickets." The pizza place next door to the Palladium is doing a brisk business and playing Elvis tunes nonstop. "Goon Squad" blares out the open door.

In a record shop two girls stare in silence for some minutes at Elvis's gawky cover photo for *My Aim Is True*. "Why is he so *sexy*?" one asks.

Now the street is just beginning to come into its own. Variety Photoplays takes on an appropriately garish aura, and the woman inside the ticket booth looks adequately macabre, as does the hooded man surreptitiously handing out flyers describing the delights within. On the

walls hang tatters of handbills and announcements. This season's movie thriller *My Bloody Valentine* crowds last holiday's *Halloween*.

By seven-thirty, the area around the Palladium is swimming with aggressive scalpers, who have a buyer's market. Elvis Costello and the "Special Attractions," as it says on the marquee, with Squeeze, have been sold out for weeks. Balcony and loge seats ($10.50) are going for $35–$49, and a good orchestra seat ($12.50) is $50–$70.

At the stage entrance in back are a motley, ragtag crew of young, well-to-do hep cats mingling with the curious street crowd, assorted freaks, the inevitable young girls, and bored, leather-jacketed youths. They wait in line, some shivering in mink, for the word from the man with the list. It is the day before the anniversary of Buddy Holly's death.

Inside, the crowd is still finding the bar, lounging in the lobby, or buying mementos from the "authorized" booth: Among the other artifacts, like the color poster of Elvis, the Attractions, and Squeeze in the studio and the white-on-black "English Mugs U.S. Tour 1981" T-shirt with Elvis's pic, there is an EP of "I Can't Stand Up (for Falling Down)" backed with "Girls Talk" that must be sending record collectors into spasms.

10

Above: The Capitol Theater. Passaic, New Jersey, February 1981. Right: On Fourteenth Street.

Recorded on the 2-Tone label (home of the Specials and Selecter) over a year ago, its release had been held up because of legal disputes between Radar, Elvis's former recording company, and Columbia. The few available discs of the original pressing of 13,000 had been selling for up to $300 each. The price here is $3.

Whatever crowd one might have expected from Fourteenth Street or Elvis Costello, this one is a fairly docile, down-jacketed group. There is also a nearly equal balance of sleazy leather jackets and unctuous polyesters. Most of the people are white, young, in the mid or late teens and early twenties, and have just the look of expectation and naivete the Union Square crowd had been hoping for.

It is Monday, February 2, 1981, the last night of Costello's visit to New York; and a few luminaries like Richard Gere, Tim Curry, and Peter Frampton have slipped in through the back door.

In the orchestra section, near the wall, an entire row of eighteen-year-old girls sits on the alert. They are lipsticked, earringed, and ready. They stand in tight pants and men's shirts, and gaze with an air of feigned ennui at the rest of the crowd. They have driven in from their school in Connecticut just for the concert and have waited so long that they are barely able to contain their excitement. The six of them sit uniformly on the edge of their seats chewing gum, chattering, and looking around,

with the exception of Carla, who sits calm and serene but is unable to conceal an occasional tremor of shivers. "Not too bad, eh?" she says, elbowing the girl next to her. "I just can't *stand* it," says her friend. "Pass the M&Ms." Later they would progress to shots of rum and tokes from a clay pipe with a flowery design in the glaze.

A string of leather jackets accompanied by two polyesters saunter down the aisle and prop themselves against the wall. A murmur runs through the crowd, then applause; and within a few minutes they are engulfed in autograph seekers and overly eager handshakers.

"What is all this?" asks Carla, staring at the throng, as she and her entourage return from the ladies' room. "It's the Ramones," someone tells her.

"The Ra-MONES!" The girls stare, mouths open, then grasp frantically for bits of paper and pens. There is a short, intense negotiation, as no one wants to go up there *by herself*; but the crowd will only allow one more to squeeze in. The appointed emissary returns triumphant with Johnny

12

Above: Actors Richard Gere (left) and Tim Curry with friends outside The Palladium.

Ramone's signature on six scraps of paper. She'd hoped for Joey's, too, but couldn't get it. "He was too spaced out," she says. Any other conclusion, including the fact that he is bearing up very well under the crush of the curious, has obviously escaped her. Meanwhile, autograph seekers have edged Johnny Ramone's miniskirted friend down the aisle, where she stands, dead-eyed and chewing gum.

Finally, the lights dim and the aisle clears as people take their seats. Johnny Ramone is heard whispering edgily to another of the group: "We told them in back we were on the guest list and he said 'Get in line.'" The crowd settles in as Squeeze takes the stage.

Squeeze is another English group best known for their singles "Pulling Mussels from a Shell" and "I Think I'm Go-Go" from *Argy-Bargy*. With lead singer Glen Tilbrook providing the main source of energy, the group has spurred a slowly growing interest in the States for their pure pop sound. They are a picture of debonair cool, dressed in the now-standard get-up of thrift-store suits and slick hair. Jools Holland, who now

13

Above: Steve Nieve (left) and Pete Thomas
enter The Palladium.

makes his own way with his Millionaires, began as their keyboardist.

"I think it's about time everybody stood up," says Tilbrook, and most of the audience complies, shouting. The Ramones and girlfriends shift against the wall, too bored or too cool to show any reaction. "Oh, come on," says Tilbrook. "There can't be two thousand people from the press here," and the group moves into a new song from their upcoming album, *East Side Story*.

Backstage, a nondescript silver bus with "Service Run" on its window has pulled up. A healthy-looking mustachioed man gets off first and scans the crowd. He sees a camera and shakes his finger naughty-naughty fashion at a photographer. "I'll take the film," he says. The photographer stands, unperturbed, and raises his flash unit. "I'll break the camera," he says, but it's too late: the Attractions are already getting off, led by bass player Bruce Thomas, followed by keyboardist Steve Nieve and drummer Pete Thomas. The beefy man goes back inside the

bus and brings back Elvis, shielding him under one arm. Cameras materialize from nowhere and a rash of flashes goes off. Elvis, looking *very* Italian, as if being taken in for income tax evasion, recoils noticeably—"Like he'd been shot" is the inevitable comment. The photographers disappear before the mustache-man has time to make good on his threats. "You know," a girl says later, "if I was him I'd do the exact same thing. He's a *commodity*."

The crowd inside has just begun to settle for the wait. Someone approaches Johnny Ramone with a telltale notebook. "I'm doing a piece on Elvis Costello," she says. "What do you think of him?"

"Never heard of the guy," he says, turning sideways. "I'm not in the band. Ask him," he says, nodding to Joey, who is slouched against the wall with his girlfriend.

She repeats the question. "Elvis who?" he says, leaning closer, the sunglasses slipping down his nose.

The woman enunciates: "EL-VIS COS-TEL-LO."

"Oh," says Joey. "Well, I'm here. That says something, doesn't it?"

"Could be professional curiosity."

"I think he's a good songwriter. Or he used to be, anyway. We'll see what he's doing now."

"Was there a particular song or album you liked?"

"I like *This Year's Model* a lot. And the first one."

"*My Aim Is True?*"

"Yeah."

"Have you ever worked with him?"

"No." Pause. "Worked with his mother once, though."

"Oh, really? How was it? You can feel free to express yourself and I won't print a word."

This rather pointless conversation comes to an end when his girlfriend says, "Look! Isn't that your lawyer?" A polyester edges by to shake hands, forcing the writer to bump rudely into Johnny Ramone's girlfriend. The writer looks for her seat, which is now occupied by Johnny Ramone. "I'll be glad to trade my seat for a quote," she says. He stands sulkily and walks away. "I really have nothing to say."

The aisles are clogged with fans trying to walk or talk off excitement. Carla and the girls are now in a huddle, passing the rum. Various red-shirted stooges run up and down the aisles, checking ticket stubs and huffing authoritatively. There is standing room only against both walls,

15

Left: Elvis and The Moustache Man (also a fan—note pin) arrive at the stage entrance.

and many have already taken up residence in the center aisles, to the indignation of those in seats; and there is a small skirmish in front center. People begin to shout, from frustration and sheer exuberance; and by the time the lights suddenly dim and the audience roars, the Palladium looks like a darkened sea of flailing arms and legs with people clambering over each other to their seats. When Elvis comes onstage, accompanied only by an acoustic guitar, the crowd is pushed over the brink from disarray to chaos. The people in the center aisles leap to their feet, blocking the view of those behind them, causing a chain reaction to the back of the theater. Soon there is a shouting match. So many in back are screaming ''Sid-DOWN'' to the jeers of those in front that it's hard to discern the fact that Costello has begun to play, much less to hear the words to the song.

It is, of course, an impossible situation. No mortal could come close to satisfying the expectations of a crowd thrown into a frenzy by weeks of charged waiting. The audience is too preoccupied with its own ire to pay attention to the man they've waited so long to see; and in the first few moments of the show, there is an unexpected role reversal. Elvis Costello, the prince of pout, the rajah of rage, sings a lullaby that goes almost unheard above the railings of those scrubbed-clean kids who were so quiet a few minutes ago. Lit by a lone spotlight, Costello opens his set with ''Gloomy Sunday,'' a 1930s hit song from Hungary. He has to be singing it for himself, because few in the audience seem prepared to listen. The ballad is about a man planning to kill himself, as the Hungarian songwriter did. It must have been something like this, one thinks, when Costello first began playing with his father in the Clubland circuit of music halls and lounges: Brawls and backroom deals hang as heavy as cigarette smoke, while the musicians play one more sweet chorus of ''Red Sails in the Sunset.''

Finally, the red-shirts eject two members of the left center aisle, to the cheers of those around them; but the moment is lost. The Attractions, led by Steve Nieve (pronounced ''naive'') take the stage; and as soon as Costello bellies up to the mike and utters the words, ''Don't ask me to apologize/I won't ask you to forgive me,'' the crowd is once again on its feet.

He looks slick, there's no doubt about that. ''Like Ronald Reagan,'' one fan had said. For this tour, anyway, he seems to have abandoned the endearing used-clothing store look for embroidered vests from the turn

16

of the century, or tonight's three-piece gray suit set off by a yellow scarf, although the especially made tour wardrobe still seems ill-fitting, given to unsightly bunches at the seams. Thank God he hasn't sold out completely, one thinks.

But the photographer who had braved the insults of Costello's entourage had it pegged exactly: "You know who he reminds me of? Roy Orbison. The glasses, the stance, everything." And sure enough, Costello has even taken on Orbison's more settled-in, grand-old-man look: He's gained a bit of weight and the hairline has receded slightly. Gone, too, are other Costello trademarks: the pigeon-toed stance, the grasping for the microphone, the distracted fingering of the eyeglasses. In fact, the show, although aptly described by Robert Palmer of the *New York Times* as a "tight, well-balanced set," borders on the mechanical. They're nearing the end of their tour and have only Boston; Providence, Rhode Island; and Passaic, New Jersey to go, after playing their way across the U.S. from the West Coast.

Costello hardly moves, except to take a drink from a cup on the organ, but the Attractions begin to loosen up. As is their practice, they keep an impossibly fast pace, tearing through the set. "Hand in Hand" sounds almost like a race. They lope into "Strict Time" from the reason for this tour, *Trust*. Costello is already glistening with perspiration.

The row of eighteen-year-old girls is undulating, some with eyes closed, and some unself-consciously dancing away. The crowd seems to have just caught on that there's a band up there: They're all still standing, but eyes are riveted onstage. The indecently young couple in front of this row have been watching without saying a word, standing without moving; but when Costello starts "You'd Better Watch Your Step" ("Don't say a word./Don't say anything..."), they look at each other and sink into their seats in a deep, long kiss. Even the rowdy boys have settled down and now just move their heads imperceptibly in time with the music. Some in the aisles are already dancing out of control, and even the Ramones seem grudgingly interested. They stand with their arms folded across their chests. Nieve, in pants so snug they look like tights, sways back and forth across the keyboard, as if waltzing. They move into "Clubland," and a backdrop of blue with white stars appears.

The mannerisms have been pared down to a nod of the head, a step from the mike, a gesture of the hand. The crowd roars its approval. The group is professional without losing the ragged edges; and when Martin

18

Belmont from Rumour and Tilbrook are added, they bring just a little more spice to the already-cooking jam. Tilbrook adds a few fancy steps, crouching down and jumping around; and he and Costello exchange many side glances throughout "From a Whisper to a Scream." Tilbrook looks young and hungry, dancing all over the stage; and when Costello says, "Isn't that kid *goot?*" it's hard to remember that Costello is only twenty-six.

The Attractions alone accompany Elvis for the encore of "Big Sister's Clothes" and "(What's So Funny 'Bout) Peace, Love and Understanding?" and the crowd lets go in a last goodbye. When the lights go up, a couple of thousand sweaty people blink at each other, resignedly put on their coats, and then begin the rap they'll tell all their friends. "More than twenty songs," says one. "I went crazy on 'Red Shoes,'" says another. "Who is that guy on the keyboards?" says Carla, her ears drawn back. "He's *great.*" The girls gather their things together to get ready for the long haul back, leaving a trail of smashed M&Ms in their wake.

In the lobby the bottleneck is effective enough to slow everyone to a crawl, giving the "authentic" booth one more shot at selling their wares. By the door, another jam: WNEW is giving out adhesive patches with Elvis's picture from *Trust* and a coupon good for two dollars off any of his albums, and the mob is reduced to grabby gimme tactics. An orderly exit is impossible—you pop out the door, as if by some trick of atmospheric pressure. Looking back, you see the sweltering maelstrom still inside; outside, there is a quiet thoroughfare of strolling twos and threes. The most enterprising of the street entrepreneurs have now made a semi-circle around the door. There's one more dose of T-shirt hawking before you step from the light under the marquee into the cold, clear night.

I Used to be Disgusted;
Now I Try to Be Amused

Elvis Costello: The name calls up a kaleidoscope of images. Punk.
Poseur. Intellectual. Bank clerk. Wimp. Angry young man. Humanist.
Racist. Anti-trendy. The new trend. Literate lyricist for the new music.
Inaccessible source to the press. Valuable commodity to a large
corporation. Famous for his scorn of the same.

Trying to pin down the Elvis Enigma is like trying to get a firm grasp on
an ice cube—at the point of most pressure it either pops from your hand,
or you look down and suddenly realize that what little you had is now
dripping through your fingers.

Which is, of course, all to his liking. It's been more than two years now
since he gave a print interview. The motives for that decision are as good
an indication as any of the dichotomy he presents his fans. Ostensibly, it's
because of the fervent "anti-rockbiz" stance that he has so far succeeded
in employing, and the reasons he's given to one or two especially trusted
writers—that he hates being pigeonholed, that much of the information
they ask for is 1) none of their business, 2) detracts from the music he
writes, 3) invites an equally detracting personal interpretation of his
lyrics, 4) is misquoted or given out of context. And last, but not least, there
is his abiding contempt for journalists, perhaps because they are the
embodiment of all the hustle, sham, and trendiness that is rockbiz. For

those reasons he has said he prefers to rely on more direct means, like television and radio, to talk to his fans rather than put himself at the mercy of a capricious reporter hungry for a story.

But at the same time, the result of all this projects an image that fits very neatly into the canon of rock history. The effect of his Garbo-like seclusion encourages endless speculation in the press, providing the glimmering outlines of legend without any of the day-to-day monotonies that might pop the bubble. And while blasting against liberal chic, he became the fave rave of that same enclave.

However, the aspects of Elvis that are agreed upon by nearly all are his amazing talent and dogged determination both to sell a lot of records and to do it his way.

You don't need to speak English to enjoy "Red Shoes" or even "Oliver's Army," but anyone who does finds a wealth of provocative material. The subjects, though presented in ordinary enough "me-and-you" form, inhabit the nether regions of human experience with sadomasochistic, violent, or fascist metaphors for everyday happenings.

24

Right: Naughty Little Elvis rocks—in leather.

It would be easy to draw a sort of Elvis cartoon from any one of the above descriptions; and it would be tempting to use such a device, if only to give a story a unified theme. But to do so would both insult the intelligence of the reader and dismantle one of Costello's most carefully laid plots: Confuse the Enemy. Divide and conquer.

It is his very inscrutability that makes him so fascinating. His actions are a part of a plan that aims at nothing less than the destruction of the Regular Way of Doing Things.

His fame itself is something of a puzzle. After the first few sessions with a wildly enthusiastic set of writers and journalists, and two very abrupt interviews in the United States, Costello refused to mete out any additional scraps to the yapping hounds. But that never stopped the press from describing him in the epigrammatic style he seems to so detest. (It is, ironically, very like the style in which he himself writes.)

Each journalist seems to have his own favorite slogan for Elvis: "The Man Who Would Be King," (Nick Kent); "Deliberately wimpy," (Ernest Leogrande); "A desperado with a guitar instead of a gun" (Tom Zito); "A British punk with a hillbilly heart" (Pete Oppel); "Communicates...the

fear of the impostor who's sure he'll be shot before he gets through his third number" (Greil Marcus); "Woody Allen sings Nietzsche...takes aim at the heart of our great depression" (Jim Miller); "Defying expectations is his business" (Tony Schwartz); "He can play Charles Bronson to his own Anthony Perkins...a rock-and-roll bounty hunter" (Kit Rachlis); "Projects the aura of a demented high-school science teacher taking a pack of juvenile delinquents on a field trip down the low road of life" *(Austin American Statesman);* "His lyrics generally explore the outer limits of the nervous system" (Bob Fixmer); "I think he has a vision of himself as an 'Avenging Dork'" (Frank Rose).

Details of Elvis's early life are scarce. His father, Ross MacManus, immigrated from Ireland at an early age. MacManus's grandfather was an Ulster Catholic, so undoubtedly Ross grew up in an area full of tension and bigotry. Ross's father, Patrick MacManus, was also a musician who came to New York to make his fortune during the Irish Rebellion in 1916. The woman Ross married, whose side of the family supplied the name Costello, came from a blue-collar area of Liverpool. Their only child, Declan Patrick MacManus, was born some twenty-seven years ago in Twickenham, London. Ross MacManus, an itinerant jazz musician once with the Joe Loss Orchestra, left to pursue his own career sometime after the family had settled in Twickenham, a blue-collar London suburb known for rugby and not much else. Declan was then about two years old.

However, it seems obvious that father and son kept in close contact. As a member of the Joe Loss Orchestra, Ross had a career that paralleled his son's early days trying to break into the music business. The seven-piece JLO first began as a relief band to the Romany Band, who were already well-established stars. In the thirties, however, the JLO began to build a reputation of its own, playing the Kit Kat Club, then returning to the Astoria as main attraction with a twelve-piece band. In the forties they led an incredible boom in wartime Palais dancing, in one week playing to 10,000 dancers at Glasgow's Playhouse Ballroom. They used the usual format, a straight singer backed by the big band, though usually the group relied on already-popular tunes rather than supplying their own. Their biggest hits were Glen Miller's "In the Mood" and Woody Herman's "Woodchopper's Ball." The Joe Loss Orchestra remained favorites of the public for forty-five years.

Ross joined the JLO in 1955 and in that same year placed tenth in a *New Musical Express (NME)* poll for big band vocalist. Reportedly,

27

Somewhere in Clubland.

Declan was brought up in a house full of jazz records; and his father knew and worked with such British jazz stars as Ronnie Scott, Phil Seamen, Joe Timperley, Tubby Hayes, and Bill McGuffie. In the early sixties Declan received his first musical education by accompanying his father to the studio to meet bands like the Stones, Hollies, Mojos, Merseybeats, and the Beatles, who were recording spots for the Joe Loss Show.

In the late sixties Ross had a German hit with "Patsy Girl" and then left the Joe Loss Orchestra in 1969. In 1970 Ross used the name "Day Costello" to cut "The Long and Winding Road" for Spark, and in the mid-seventies sported longish hair, satin trousers, and hippy shirts. These days he makes his living on the northern cabaret circuit, with a schedule perhaps even more grueling than his son's. The two sometimes meet at Watford Gap when their tours crisscross and some years ago appeared together in a lemonade commercial, with Elvis providing guitar and backing vocals and Ross playing piano and supplying lead vocals.

Undoubtedly some of the most valuable lessons Declan learned from his father were about the inside workings of the business. Thus armed, Elvis very effectively short-circuited the usual years-of-playing-in-obscurity-followed-by-one-hit-single-and-promptly-dismissed-a-year-later cycle that is the usual story of rock & roll. Part of the value of his father's experience was that Elvis would go into the business with eyes open, shorn of any illusions about stardom. In fact, it seems that by the time he finally began to make it, his anger at the fact that he'd done it in spite of the still-existing old-boy structure, that he was an exception and had done very little to really upset people, kept him going. He harbored no glamourous ideas about the glories of being a musician. He told Mick Brown that his father had discouraged him from entering the business, that it was "something you do in spite of your better judgment."

Declan was raised a Catholic ("I had to be Catholic or Jewish, now didn't I?" he told Nick Kent of *NME*); and according to statements by both Elvis and his father, one of the most important early lessons of his childhood was his mother's insistence on accepting the equality of his neighbors in the multiracial area. "It wasn't just something on the side," Ross told *NME*. "It was a central issue."

Somewhere along the line he acquired his first "favorite" record, "Please Please Me" by the Beatles. Although he was only about ten when the record came out, it must have been vastly impressive to have been so close to the source of the four lads who were about to conquer the world.

He left school at sixteen, in 1971, but not before meeting the girl, Mary, who would become his wife. He went directly to Liverpool, one of the few places he seems to like.

When he first began giving interviews, Elvis told the questioners that he'd worn the same kind of clothes for years and that one reason his anger was unleashed in America was that "everyone looked at us as if we came from Mars." It's easy to imagine the same Elvis, awkward and unremarkable at twelve, six, or even as a gap-toothed and bespectacled infant. In spite of the popular impression that Elvis and the Attractions suddenly veered into view out of left field, close reading of interviews reveals his single-minded pursuit of an outlet for his songs for years before he was finally signed. And in spite of the amazing speed with which the public accepted him, he would always complain that the process was too slow.

People found it hard to believe that Elvis was just twenty-two when he emerged on London's horizon, and, in fact, he has said that when he was eighteen he felt thirty, with the deadly cynicism of an embittered old man.

His first loves in music were jazz and country—mostly country. After leaving Twickenham for Liverpool, he worked at a variety of odd jobs while fine-tuning his songwriting skills. He would later describe most of these early songs to Robert Hilburn as "almost obsessively uncommercial." It wasn't until after he found Stiff that he "went beserk," he says, and started writing popular songs. It was hopeless to expect anyone to accept a country musician from England. But he cultivated a great respect for a variety of musicians ranging from Dusty Springfield to Joni Mitchell to the Damned, and later showed that he'd avidly studied their techniques, speaking knowledgeably about the "emotionless" jazz singers and their opposites who mike emotion from every line. George Jones would remain one of Costello's steadfast favorites. Even Lorenz and Hart are among the admired songwriters.

While he was in Liverpool, he first began making his way as a "semi-professional" under the name D. P. Costello. One night backstage at Eric's in Liverpool, he struck up a conversation with Nick Lowe, the bassist of pub rock kings Brinsley Schwarz. The two became friends, meeting again at the Cavern Club. When Costello began making trips to London, Lowe put him up on the floor of his flat. For a time, according to Lowe, Costello roadied for the Brinsleys.

When he was nineteen, he moved back to London to take a message to Mary. They married, settling in Whitton, Middlesex, and by the time their son, Matthew, was born, Costello was working at Elizabeth Arden in Acton (the "vanity factory" of "I'm Not Angry") as a computer operator. Although some fans envisioned a semi-mutant computer whiz when that story leaked, Costello made it clear that the job was "more a hobby" for which he was paid £20 a week. He used the company stationery and phone to peddle his work. His bluegrass band, Flip City, had become a sort of house band for London's Marquee, which, like New York's CBGB, was originally dedicated to folk music but eventually became a regular stopover for the sweatier new bands.

He had sent tapes to every major recording company, and when those efforts produced nothing, he decided that a face-to-face confrontation might be the best bet. (He later claimed his motives were probably based on having watched too many old movies.) Guitar case in hand, he hit the streets. Somehow managing to weasel his way into executives' offices, he installed himself inside, refusing to be ignored. Singing away while cigar-chewing businessmen alternated between calls on lines three and four, however, produced little reaction other than their irritation.

Impatience soon turned to bitterness. Obviously, the execs had no idea of what to make of this hand-me-down Holly. What, no glitter? No subservience? No blue moon/coke spoon? Oswald MOSLEY???

Just as he'd exhausted the last of his hopes, he saw an advertisement from a small London record company looking for new artists. Declan's tape was the first one Jake Riviera received at the new company, Stiff Records ("If they're dead, we'll sign 'em.")

30

Right: "I could never imagine a lot of people wanting this ugly geek in glasses ramming his songs down their throats."

Moods for Moderns

In March of 1981, the intrepid Tom Snyder followed his scoop interview with Elvis by treating network TV to the presence of the Plasmatics, whose lead singer, Wendy O. Williams, had just stirred yet another to-do in the rock press by her arrest for obscenity in Snyder's beloved home town of Milwaukee. They performed their standard set, punctuated by Williams's smashing a TV and bisecting a guitar with a chain saw. The bikini-clad Williams then stepped from the stage to answer questions from a puzzled and twitching Snyder, the set smouldering in the background. "After all," she said, "rock & roll has always been an *attitude.*"

Nevertheless, when the new bands burst on the scene looking like so many ragged anorectics, destruction gleaming from narrowed eyes, the reaction ranged from sheer glee to abject terror. A word about words: A desperate attempt to pin down "what it all means" (which perhaps preoccupied Americans more than the English) resulted in the coinage of the vague terms "punk" and "new wave." "Punk" was easily recognizable: Snarls and safety pins were dead giveaways. But as more diverse bands followed in the wake of that short-lived trend, "new wave" took over. A loose definition might include a concentration on the energy of early rock & roll, as well as some of the clothes, a good dose of humor, or simply anything the record industry or the press could not categorize as anything else.

In fact, the rise of the new wave can be traced in a nearly continuous line from the earliest days of rock & roll, with direct influence from the pioneers: even Presley used to sneer. The best aspects of the beginnings—the good-time three-chord single, go-go boots, and frightened parents—are all important elements.

In an interview, Costello compared 1977 to 1966, the year of heady, top-down, 60-m.p.h. rock, when the Beatles were at their peak and a veritable fleet of new bands careened toward the public eye. Bill Graham had just opened the doors to the Fillmore, and soon psychedelia would have the nation in the grip of vertigo. The British invasion had spurred an unprecedented interest in the teen market, and before long everyone was in the act. Rockbiz was born.

But even while Martha and the Vandellas were still putting their stamp on AM's reign of power in 1966, one group was formed that is most pointed to as the earliest new-wave forerunner—the Velvet Underground, with songwriter Lou Reed on guitar and John Cale on electric viola, whose lyrics (described by *The New Music* as "documentary realism...about urban decay and heroin addiction") attracted the attention of Andy Warhol. They became a part of his "Exploding Plastic Inevitable" avant-garde mixed-media show and released their album, *White Light/White Heat*, in 1967 on Verve Records.

Meanwhile, in the Midwest, professional madman Iggy Pop and his Detroit Stooges surfaced, to the horror of Michigan's concerned moms and dads. And on the West Coast the Flamin' Groovies emerged as near-polar images of hippie culture, and by releasing their own 10-inch album, *Sneakers*, opened the way for the very important, do-it-yourself record and resurgence of the "indies"—independently produced records. A few years later, Costello cohort Dave Edmunds would produce singles for them.

In 1971 the New York Dolls materialized, teetering on platform heels and leaving a trail of ostrich feathers from their boas. Although their fame was brief, their influence was electric, and on a last tour of Japan they were accompanied by Richard Hell, later of Television. Their 1974 visit to England attracted the attention of Malcolm McLaren, who managed them before turning to that great rock & roll swindle, the Sex Pistols.

In the mid-sixties, British mods, predominantly white kids obsessively fashion conscious and born to dance, found an unlikely ally in the form of the influx of Jamaican reggae, a direct descendant of ska and bluebeat.

34

Right: Renegades from Live Stiffs: Ian Dury and The Blockheads.

Ska and bluebeat gave birth to the first truly cross-cultural bands, mixing black and white, male and female. Their undeniable starting point lies with Bob Marley and the Wailers, and developed to include bands like Selecter, the Specials, the Bodysnatchers, and Madness, all characterized by a stage teeming with wildly gyrating members in crew cuts, baggy pants, and felt fedoras.

In England the early seventies saw the rise of two more of the many factions bubbling ominously beneath the surface of rock culture: glitter rock, with the concentration on sham, costumes, and theatrics (David Bowie, T. Rex, Gary Glitter, and later Mott the Hoople and Roxy Music); and pub rock. Some of the more easily recognizable names of the English new wave established themselves after long years of barely supporting themselves in the rounds of intimate, sweaty clubs across the country. Dr. Feelgood, the Kursaal Flyers, Kilburn and the High Roads (with lead singer Ian Dury), Brinsley Schwarz (Nick Lowe, Ian Gomm, Bob Andrews, Brinsley Schwarz, Billy Rankin), Ducks Deluxe (Martin Belmont, who went with Andrews to Graham Parker's Rumour), Love Sculpture (David Edmunds, who, with Nick Lowe, formed Rockpile), Chilli Willi and the Red Hot Peppers (with Pete Thomas of the Attractions and managed by one Jake Riviera) were among them. Soon the atmosphere cultivated an even younger, hotter dance craze, with the

Nick Lowe.

likes of Eddie and the Hot Rods and Wreckless Eric calling the steps, thus setting the stage for Elvis's entrance.

But the mass marketplace was a different story, and marketing techniques and technological advances had as much to do with the history of rock as any garage band singer with two-toned shoes. With the almighty influence of megabucks, the scene had taken on a perverse irony: Rock concerts became multimedia debacles for immense crowds (if in fact, the groups toured at all—the Stones and the Who were in semiretirement and the Beatles disbanded); the FCC's decision to bail out ailing FM stations by providing them with stereo, album-oriented airplay took hold, and the "theme" album nudged out the single. Also, newer, cheaper, better stereo home equipment from the Japanese created a whole new breed of hi-fi snobs who dedicated endless hours to filtering the last bit of distortion from their albums. In the United States especially, the post-psychedelic era's playlists were ruled by groups more interested in high-gloss technique and epic spectacle than back seat romance.

36

Wreckless Eric.

Pink Floyd, Queen, and Emerson, Lake and Palmer were typical; and ELP's concert climax—in which Keith Emerson and his white baby grand were suspended high above the stage and slowly upended in a somersault above the crowd—proved that the spectacle had just about been stretched to its limit.

England, too, was suffering through its own miasma, with the Bay City Rollers playing to the United States's disco craze. Even *Melody Maker* and *NME* followed their actions closely, but their interest lay more with the wistful nostalgia the Rollers brought by enticing young girls to scream once more. Even Lowe momentarily lost his cool and recorded "Goin' to See the Rollers."

Typically, as big business, the record industry in the United States was highly reluctant to take a gamble on the new bands struggling to make it. They didn't ask for much from a rock band—only that they fit into the already safe and familiar formula of a group that could pack Madison Square Garden. And, typically, the executives rarely recognized such a

37

group when it *did* come along. More significantly, the independent labels that had given the public groups like Frankie Lymon and the Teenagers had either grown into a miniature industry themselves (like Atlantic) or undergone threat of extinction because of a lack of promotional power to compete with the majors.

Fortunately, U.K. record buyers and makers seemed much more open to the new; otherwise, American artists from Jimi Hendrix to the Ramones might have starved. True, it is a much more fashion-conscious, openly trendy process in which yesterday's marvel bands are discarded like so much Kleenex; but two independent labels, Chiswick and Stiff, formed by Dave Robinson and the man who would later become Costello's manager, Jake Riviera, backed with a loan from Dr. Feelgood, gave the majors a real run for their money. The only equivalent in the United States was the mail-order setup Beserkeley Records, whose LP, *Beserkely Chartbusters*, gave the world its first taste of Jonathan Richman's Modern Lovers.

Meanwhile, America's tastes in the seventies reflected a stultifying sameness: The Bee Gees topped the charts time and again. And while the pub rock scene firmly established itself around the country, the U.S.

38

Above: Elvis with stand-in bass player, Phil Lynott. April 1978.

equivalent was based down, down, downtown in the Bowery of New York City, in the crumbling edifice, wedged between a flophouse and mounds of garbage, known as CBGB, where Patti Smith had found an outlet for her poetry readings and rock & roll. It opened in 1974, when manager Hilly Kristal took pity on bands that would establish themselves at the forefront of the American new wave. "Where else can they play?" he asked. House regulars included the Stilettos (whose girl singer Debbie Harry would return with Blondie), the Talking Heads, Television, the Heartbreakers (with Jerry Nolan of the New York Dolls), and that seminal voice of change, The Ramones.

The Ramones' main forte is the nasty pop single, and by stubbornly clinging to the adolescent ideals of energy and throwaway lyrics coupled with urban boredom, they produced such blatantly simple-minded classics as "Suzy is a Headbanger," "Sheena is a Punk Rocker," "Sniffin' Glue," "Cretin Hop," and, of course, "I Wanna Be Sedated."

The cyclical nature of pop music has already been well documented, but the facts bear one more once-over. Here, as in England, the rise of creativity in pop music seems to be connected to political turbulence. Witness 1968 in the United States: the Democratic National Convention; the Chicago Seven; the Tet Offensive; the assassinations of Robert Kennedy and Martin Luther King; Richard Nixon's rise to power; George Wallace coming on strong. But the gold records that year are a glittering array of gems: Aretha Franklin's "Chain of Fools," "Judy in Disguise with Glasses" by John Fred and the Playboys, Dionne Warwicke's "I Say A Little Prayer," Otis Redding's "Sittin' on the Dock of the Bay," "Tighten Up" by Archie Bell and the Drells, "Hello I Love You" by the Doors. The baby boom was losing its baby fat and didn't much like what it saw of the adult world. There was a surge toward the innocuous—Gary Lewis and the Playboys, the Monkees, and 1910 Fruitgum Company were all powerful messages from today's youth. The music had taken on more sophistication with the arrival of Crosby, Stills and Nash, Jimi Hendrix, and Janis Joplin; but those prepubescent kids itching at home, playing the hi-fi while big sister went to the National Guard Armory to see Jerry Lee Lewis, would suddenly find themselves out of high school with no such movement of their own. They'd missed the eye liner, the sock hops, the protests; and now even that bastion of American teen influence, the automobile, was becoming an endangered species. The waning numbers of the baby boom took on the last few wisps of hippiedom, bearing frayed jeans and jackets almost apologetically, but embraced another legacy—drugs—far more enthusiastically. The next generation was in danger of becoming a glassy-eyed postscript.

The seventies saw the end of upheaval, the end of the revolution, the end of many rock stars' lives. The Woodstock generation went to work, and soon the numbing influence of disco set in. By 1975 it was a most self-conscious affliction: The rock press complained endlessly about the pervasive sterility. "Rock and roll is dead," said Todd Rundgren. He was actually one reason why it was being kept alive; he was the producer of the Dolls' 1973 album.

But as the flower children resigned themselves to Wall Street and became part of the Silent Majority, unrest was on the rise in England, from a combination of post-Empire welfare-state blues complicated by the growing "immigration problem"—in fact a seething undercurrent of racial strife. England's recession and unemployment offered little hope to the coming generation and the brewing discontent mothered a like breeding ground for new talent. The Profumo scandal had created the same longing for entertainment as the aftermath of the Kennedy assassination did in the United States in 1964.

As early as 1954, when playwright John Osborne's *Look Back in Anger* (also the title of a Bowie song) premiered, the "angry young man" had found a voice for his disenchantment on English stages. Critics burned Osborne for his sordid characters, seedy setting, apparent misogyny, and self-defeating rage; but it was a sort of early punk play, which gave the momentum for the "new-wave" theater of Joe Orton, Harold Pinter, et al.

Meanwhile, one D. P. Costello and his bluegrass band, Flip City, picked away in obscurity at their regular dates at London's Marquee.

It was the Flamin' Groovies debut in England in 1976 that would really spark that nation, which was already on the brink of change, to coalesce all the splintered movements of pub rock and punk. Ironically, it was not the Flamin' Groovies, who were responsible for this momentous occasion, but their opening act—the Ramones—whose blithely snotty, two-chord set instantaneously galvanized London.

Already the movement was a year old. The Sex Pistols had opened in November of 1975. The Naughty Rhythms tour had set the stage for the package tour (with Dr. Feelgood, Nick Lowe and Dave Edmunds, and Chilli Willi and the Red Hot Peppers alternating as headliners) and

proved profitable. London clubs like the Vortex and the Marquee opened their doors to punks, and shoestring fanzines started fanning the fires.

Nick Lowe's 45, "So It Goes" b/w "Heart of the City," was the first to prove there was still a market out there for the "song." The first European Punk Rock Festival, held in August, featured Lowe, the Damned, and the Hot Rods. But the Damned were the first to release a punk LP, also on Stiff in 1976, and Riviera followed up this threat by taking them on the first punk tour of the United States soon afterward.

But, of course, all this was a prelude to the screaming riot caused by the Sex Pistols.

Living proof that hype can be stranger than fiction, the Pistols were recruited by Malcolm McLaren, owner of a punk boutique on King's Road called Sex, from the group Swankers. Bassist Steve Jones dubbed Johnny Lydon "Johnny Rotten" because of the virgin green scum on his teeth, untouched by a toothbrush. Sid Vicious, hired after Matlock was fired, had played with the Flowers of Romance (later the name of a PiL album) and Siouxsie and the Banshees. He earned his spot on the basis of a performance in the shop lip-synching to Alice Cooper's "I'm Eighteen." The Sex Pistols would return the States's favor of the Ramones's tour with a vengeance.

Their short career was an amazing entanglement of drugs, recording contracts, and brushes with the law. Some highlights: Goaded into

uttering obscenities on ITV's "Today" show, the Pistol's resulting media uproar gave them their first real push. Eventually signed by giant EMI, their "Anarchy in the U.K." was an anthem for the streets' lost souls. "God Save the Queen (and Her Fascist Regime)" reached number two on the U.K. charts during the Queen's Silver Jubilee, in spite of the fact that it was banned from radio airplay. Dumped by EMI in the midst of controversy and forbidden to play by local councils, the Pistols went underground as the Spots (Sex Pistols On Tour Secretly) and continued hitting the small club circuit. When they finally toured the U.S., they scorned the center of hipdom, New York, and went directly to the redneck, beer-belly underpinnings in Georgia and Texas.

Soon the pressures of the tour caused rifts of every imaginable type, between McLaren and Rotten, Vicious and Rotten, and the group broke up in San Francisco, their last stop. Vicious survived his first OD on heroin on the plane ride back to New York. (His condition is painfully obvious in the Sid Vicious–Nancy Spungeon interview in Lech Kowalski's documentary, *D.O.A.*—unable to keep from nodding out and burning Nancy with cigarettes even as he tries answering questions. Supposedly, the camera crew had rushed over when Nancy Spungeon called and said, "Come interview Sid. We think he's gonna die.")

Rotten went back to Johnny Lydon and formed Public Image Ltd.; McLaren's latest enterprise is capitalizing on the tape piracy scam with his new band Bow Wow Wow, and the rest of the group went down to South America to seek a new vocalist in the form of Ronald Biggs, the Great Train Robber. Sid went on to be charged with Nancy's murder in

42

Above: The Hope and Anchor, London.

their New York Chelsea Hotel room and eventually died of an overdose of heroin in February 1979.

Even now much of their music is misinterpreted: The media excitement all but blotted out the fact that many of their songs were almost impossibly idealistic, not reflecting the hopeless nihilism most connect with them. One of Lydon's songs is a forceful attack on abortion; the verse of another urges, "Be somebody."

But their effect on the media was just as important: They stood the international press on its ear for the first time in years. The rock press was in an orgasmic frenzy trying to keep up with the new bands, many of whom spurned the media.

But after all the tragic waste and misinterpretation, the final lasting effect of the Sex Pistols was the catharsis needed to get teens away from the TV and back in bands. The new wave was born; and the groups emerged, wearing black leather, spandex, stilettos, purple hair, blue lips, and thrift-store suits. They bore names from the back pages of comic books: X-Ray Specs, B-Girls, Bizarros, Blondie; distressing verbs: the Clash, the Cramps, Squeeze, the Jam; threatening eminences: the B-52's, the Piranhas, Police, Shrapnel, the Lurkers, Buzzcocks, the Damned, Dictators, They Must Be Russians, Gang of Four; common-as-dirt nouns: the Shirts, the Shoes, the Boys, Motels, Motors, the Cars, the Knack, the Humans, the Waitresses, Kleenex, Pylon, the Members; revolting images: the Dead Kennedys (with lead singer Jello Biafra), Boomtown Rats, the Brains, Dead Boys, Sick Fucks, Stiff Little Fingers, Teenage Jesus and the Jerks, Suicide, Tampax; technological terms: Human Switchboard, Talking Heads, the Void-Oids, Androids, Television, Telephone, Radiators from Space, Magnetic Head Cleaners, Tiny Desk Unit; oxymorons: Urban Verbs, Desperate Bicycles, Bush Tetras, Flying Lizards, Exploding Seagulls, Insect Surfers, Leather Nun, Throbbing Gristle, Disturbed Furniture, Young Marble Giants; and those whose names could only be described as stoo-pud: Jog and the Tracksuits, the Dickheads, Splodgeness Abounds, Swell Maps, Money for Drugs.

Groups like Blondie, the B-52's, the Clash, and our man Elvis, having shown the record companies wot's wot, no longer eke out a living on the small club circuit; they've taken their place leading the music of a young decade. It will be interesting to see what develops from here. With groups like Adam and the Ants causing the most discussion in the rock press today, one might speculate that we're in for another round of the cycle.

I Want to Bite
the Hand That Feeds Me

Jake Riviera (né Andrew Jakeman), an ex-adman from Pinner, got the idea of forming his own label after taking the Feelgoods on their first U.S. tour in 1974. He was managing Chilli Willi and the Red Hot Peppers, an eccentric group whose album *Bongoes over Balham* on Moonbeam was a sign of things to come. In thrift shops he saw the myriad labels born of get-rich-quick schemes and probably dying just as fast. He later told *Melody Maker* reporter Alan Jones, "I spent years shouting at people over desks in record company offices. They turned down virtually every idea I had."

Somewhere in the Louisiana bayous, the idea probably rose like swamp gas: Why not form a record company of his own? By the time the tour (a flop) was over, he'd figured out the slogans, the logo, and the name: Stiff Records was born.

A number of people, including Elvis, have said, in effect, that Jake Riviera was Stiff Records. Abrasive, no-nonsense, always seeming to enjoy himself enormously even as he squelched some poor reporter's hopes for an interview ("I'm not interested that you're interested"), Riviera's antics were apparently his own best entertainment. Even Stiff's rejection letters conveyed a cheery bluntness. A large "REJECTION" stamped across the left-hand corner, the letter closed with "Thanks for sending it in anyway and don't give up, even though the best record company has in fact turned you down...." Early interviews reveal a canny businessman with a shocking attitude (considering the industry) of respect for "the kids."

"Kids are hipper and brighter than most record companies think. Stiff is interested in reaching those kids, right. I'm not interested in handing out stacks of free records and T-shirts and free lunches to journalists and dealers. I'm interested in the kids who buy the records, not the music business. And I want to offer those kids a good deal," he told Jones.

He is Costello's perfect complement. Given to Western shirts and cowboy boots pointy enough to impale any kitchen-corner roach, Riviera seemed only too willing to enforce his client's wishes to remain above the frenzied workings of rockbiz. Writers and photographers were given implicit warnings, and when they resorted to the time-tested method of hustling for a story, Riviera made good on his threats. In time his reputation as Costello's strong-arm was perhaps overblown, but Costello capitalized on the image, with references to "the bully boys out/changing someone's facial design" (*Hand in Hand*).

Costello is far from apologetic for Riviera. "I've tried being reasonable," he said in an interview printed in *Wet* magazine. "It means you have to be nice to people you hate."

Yet even as reporters felt the heat of Riviera's wrath (Jones says Riviera reminds him of a "hip Hitler"), they were nearly always equally intrigued by his candor. Even as Riviera hoisted Charlie Crespo by his lapels to emphasize his contempt of American rockbiz, the reporter said he really felt no fear. It had something to do with the prankster's gleam in Riviera's eyes.

Procuring a loan from the Feelgoods, Riviera and partner Dave Robinson set up Stiff and Avancedale Management, which handled the careers of Graham Parker and the Rumour, Elvis, Clover (the backup band on *My Aim Is True*), Nick Lowe, and the Damned. (Robinson was also apparently behind the embarrassing "Fillmore Hype" incident, in which Famepushers Ltd. had flown a planeload of reporters to witness Brinsley Schwarz's opening—one of their less remarkable performances.)

Graham Parker, who was frequently compared to Elvis in early reviews, along with Bruce Springsteen and Bob Dylan, had begun his career at almost exactly the same time, so articles stating that Parker was an obvious influence provided yet another irritation to an already-chafed

An early Stiff poster.

Elvis. Also, according to Elvis in *NME*, Robinson had once granted studio time to both him and Parker, and, at about the same time, to an American, John Borsay, who later changed his name to Willy DeVille. Yet another "influence" bites the dust.

Establishing a hold on London's West Side on the ground floor of a building behind Porchester Road and Westbourne Grove, a core of six residents would make up the Stiff "family": Cynthia Cole, Riviera's right hand; Suzanne Spire; art director Barney Bubbles; general manager Paul Conroy; Robinson; and Riviera.

The self-proclaimed "undertakers to the industry," Stiff's greatest strengths were knowing where the talent was and cutting through red tape to get to the business of distributing records. Stiff was one of the first labels, along with Chiswick, Skydog in France, and Dynamo in Holland, to concentrate on the then-anemic singles market. As the new music erupted, indie labels sprang up with them like mushrooms overnight, seemingly one for every new band. Many of them took their cue from Stiff, which led the way with picture sleeves, gimmicky promos (including scores of catchy but slightly twisted slogans), and giveaway copies.

Soon every brainstorm found an outlet: singles were pressed on blue, red, or yellow vinyl, on triangles, picture discs, 7- and 12-inch EPs. These indies were marked contrasts to their U.S. equivalents, averaging sales of up to 30,000 for quality singles—sometimes without the boost of radio attention. U.S. singles averaged about 7,000 across the vast continent.

Ian Dury's "Hit Me With Your Rhythm Stick" on Stiff eventually sold a million copies. The American exceptions were Patti Smith's "Piss Factory" on Mer and Richard Hell's *Blank Generation* EP. The B-52's, Pylon, and the Rubinoos also found their audiences through the indie.

Within two years, Stiff would challenge the biggies. Riviera, however, thought the biggies' chances for success were dubious. "I feel sorry for all these overweight executives....They take an idea and sterilize it out of existence." He would be more specific to Mick Brown, saying that most executives "are complete dinks who wouldn't know good music if it bit them in the arse."

But even Riviera was caught off guard by the excellence of D. P. Costello's home-cooked acoustical arrangement on tape. As it was the first tape he received, he had no means of comparison. He called Costello and told him he thought it sounded good, but he needed a little

Above: Practicing anonymity.

more time. When subsequent tapes brought "a load of real dross" and Lowe and the others agreed the tape sounded great, Riviera signed him up in early 1977.

The first change was made: in a West London bar, Jake christened him anew: Now there was a skinny Elvis again. It was, of course, provocative. Some took immediate offense at the sheer nerve of borrowing the name of a rock idol whose legend was close to canon in the eyes of his fans, and especially when the new Elvis was such an antisexy troublemaker. Presley was still alive at the time. (Incredibly, the name would later take still one more mutation with the appearance of another new wave London artist, one "Elton Motello.")

As reported in Nick Kent's 1979 *NME* interview, Stiff placed another ad, this time requesting members of a "pop combo." Extensive auditions were held to locate a band, with Andrew Bodnar of the Rumour in attendance. Pete Thomas, drummer in the first band Riviera handled, the Chillis, had stayed in the United States after the tour, working with folk singer John Stewart on the West Coast. Dissatisfied with that position and hearing the reports of the new music back home, he returned, this time to have a try at a group with former Chillis bassman Paul Riley, and Wilko Johnson, who had left the Feelgoods. That lasted only a week, but Riviera beckoned. With Bruce, Pete would supply the bedrock of experience in the Attractions.

Like Pete Thomas, Bruce Thomas (no relation), bassist from the Sutherland Brothers and Quiver, and a short-lived group called Moonrider, also had a strong reputation from these groups as well as from session work. It was this reputation that survived an abrupt conversation with Elvis, when he asked what groups Bruce liked. "I replied that I liked Graham Parker and a couple of Steely Dan albums. Elvis immediately said, 'Forget it,'" he told Kent. Someone else arranged for an audition. "I've always wanted to be a member of...y'know...*the* group, the greatest band," he said. Bruce's wonderfully spare arrangements have sometimes even taken a position at the forefront—almost a lead bass.

Steve Nieve was the last member signed. Although he had no professional experience, his contribution to the Attractions is arguably the most distinctive and over the span of five albums shows the greatest range, from the primitive, delightfully honky Farfisa to the grand scope and tinkly cocktail sophistication on *Trust*. He is the perfect counterpoint to the firm anchor that Thomas and Thomas provide.

Left: A classic portrait a la Hank Williams.

Like Costello and Riviera, Nieve also took on a pseudonym, and his is a more precise summation of his personality as described by Kent: "disarming…almost languishing in his reputation as an innocent young cove." His name has been listed as "Steve Young" and "Steve Adore" as well as Nason, Mason, Manson, Hart, Naive, finally becoming Nieve, as listed on the albums. A student at the Royal College of Music, he claimed he owned only two rock albums—T. Rex and Alice Cooper—and that he'd never heard of "? and the Mysterons," as he called them.

"I really don't understand why we're not as big as the Bay City Rollers," he told Kent; and although Kent called this attitude "ridiculous," it was one that Elvis would echo in statement and style. Nieve's favorite musician was Michel Legrand, and he said he'd like to write movie scores. His fave would be something like "Love story." Although he professed confusion at some of Elvis's music (!), he said he liked it best "when it gets weird and spooky."

Although no dates are given for the group's formation, presumably they assembled sometime after the taping of *My Aim Is True*, done in the simple, eight-track Pathway Studios in Highbury on a shoestring budget with Clover in early 1977 and released in July. The album's release was reportedly delayed for some months while Stiff and Island wrangled over a distribution deal. The first single, "Less Than Zero" b/w "Radio Sweetheart," was released in March; and "Alison" b/w "Welcome to the Working Week" followed in May. (Note: Record release dates are based on the best available sources. See Discography.)

Some of Elvis's early singles were deleted almost immediately, but "Less Than Zero" began to catch. Inspired by a television program's attempt to put Hitlerite Oswald Mosley "in perspective," "Zero" was at once a put-down of fascist longings and liberal chic. According to Costello, the program's position of "it was all forty years ago anyway" was what sparked his anger at a growing complacency. Mosley's admirers in the National Front took considerable offense, but Costello was soon working on another song sending up the bullyboys, "Night Rally." And when he found out that the Yanks thought the song was about Lee Harvey Oswald, he promptly supplied "Less Than Zero's" "Dallas Version."

Seventy-seven was a halcyon year for the motley, ragtag crew at Stiff. The first Stiff compilation album, *A Bunch of Stiffs*, released in April of 1977, contained Elvis's "Less Than Zero" and eleven singles and outtakes from the rest of Stiff's glittering array of talent: Nick Lowe, Motorhead,

52

The UK picture sleeve for Accidents will Happen *was printed inside out. Sleeve is split here to show graphics.*

Magic Michael, Wreckless Eric, Dave Edmunds, Stones Masonry, and a group called The Takeaways, with a mystery singer lampooning Dylan.

"Unwind City Begins If You Buy This Album Now" and "Contains No Hit Single Whatsoever" were Stiff's slogans for the next Stiff compilation, *Hits Greatest Stiffs*, and Riviera's sales tactics worked well. Productions costs were low and distribution efficient.

The Live Stiffs tour was a sort of new wave "Meet the Beatles," with the outlying areas of the U.K. getting their first glimpses of Lowe, Eric, Wallis, and Elvis, and resulted in the *Live Stiffs* compilation. Based on the Naughty Rhythms alternating headliners formula, it was a smashing success, stretching from the High Wycombe town hall through Bristol, Liverpool, Glasgow, Sheffield, Leicester, and ending at Lancaster University. Already Costello was proving testy, refusing to rely on the few singles the audience may have known and breaking out with all-new material. The release of "Watching the Detectives" (the first with the Attractions) followed soon afterward, and finally, also in August, *My Aim Is True*. Riviera reportedly brought Stiff to the brink of bankruptcy buying ads for the album.

53

In the meantime, Elvis's solo performances were the sites of near-riots. At the Nashville, 700 angry fans were turned away. Costello had begun using his "little black book," personally trimming the guest list of unwanted Island execs and others. He told Kent that he also kept track of those he gave passes and didn't show.

Yet this wasn't quite enough. Some of the local papers had shown a nibbling interest in Costello, although they seemed as unprepared for the unlikely looking rock star as their U.S. counterparts would later. The Live Stiffs tour had generated a good deal of interest in the rock press, and Riviera concocted a plan of action to follow it up.

CBS was holding a convention for its record execs at the London Hilton. Since the late sixties, Columbia had acquired a reputation as the stronghold of the industry music scene. Jake's plan was again to confront them directly, as Elvis had done so many times before. Elvis would serenade them as they returned from their lunch break.

The episode, described in an August 1977 *Melody Maker*, had all the elements of a Judy Garland–Mickey Rooney "I know! Let's put on a show!" movie plot. Riviera dispatched Graham Parker roadies Kosmo and Alphonse, wearing Stiff sandwich boards, to the scene. Riviera, sipping cider, was his usual ebullient self, as Elvis plugged in the Vox practice amp Riviera had given him as part of an advance and launched "Welcome to the Working Week" before a generally delighted group of passersby and one displeased concierge. When his requests for Elvis to move were ignored, he went inside to call the police.

By the time the execs appeared, there was a crowd of perhaps fifty, including one tourist who requested a Neil Diamond number. The execs, including CBS prez Walter Yetnikoff, stopped and were soon tapping their feet and clapping their hands like the rest of the crowd. However, the fact that Elvis was simply singing, not busking, did not deter the young inspector who arrived. "Move on, son," said the inspector, according to *Melody Maker*. Elvis did one sidestep and continued.

"Right," said the officer. "You're nicked."

This was not part of the plan. Riviera was again in action, this time to "spring Elvis" ("He's got a sound check at Dingwall's at four!").

Elvis, duly sprung, reported he expected to pay a £5 fine for obstruction and requested that a copy of his album be sent to the station.

True to the Judy-Mickey form, the scheme worked. He was signed by Columbia.

I'm Here to Corrupt America's Youth

The summer of 1977 came to a close, and for a while, Lowe, Dury, and the rest of the Stiff enclave took to hanging around Riviera's offices. Journalists' oft repeated speculations that Costello must have known what was coming are correct: He was frequently spotted there in some empty office, an unassuming figure made nearly invisible by the newspaper he held, simply waiting. Picture Elvis going home, another anonymous clerk with the paper under his arm, and emerging again in one of London's steamy clubs, whipping the crowd (and himself) into a spastic frenzy, escaping through back doors and greeting the established rockbiz writers and businessmen waiting there with a snarl. Welcome to the working week.

He was on the brink of becoming a household Elvis, and his little black book was teeming with the names of those who'd found it convenient to ignore him. Riviera turned his inimitable talents to the promotion of *My Aim Is True*: Full-page ads appeared in England's three biggest music mags, *Melody Maker, New Musical Express*, and *Record Mirror*, each with one-third of the album cover pic. Fans who wanted the whole picture had to buy all three. American ads included one with Elvis's album cover pose, pigeon-toed and squinting, over the phrase "Reality Was Never This Good." Riviera's publicity, which had always verged on a "We don't need you. We don't *want* you" approach, attracted buyers in droves. Riviera also sponsored a "Help Us Hype Elvis" giveaway.

In October, at the height of the Live Stiffs tour, Riviera, saying he was becoming "bored" with the label, decided to throw in his lot with Elvis, accompanying him to Columbia as manager. The parting of ways between co-founder Dave Robinson and Riviera was described as "amicable." Riviera would later say that Stiff was on the way to becoming another major label and was no longer a challenge.

From then on Elvis, Lowe, and Riviera would be inseparable allies in mischief responsible for Costello's career. The trio had enjoyed a moderate degree of recognition (or, in Jake's case, notoriety), but somehow their combination of quirks resulted in just the effort needed to boost them from cult status to prominence allied with the merry ring of cash registers. All three relish the pun, the twisted cliche, and when their oddball humor found its way to the marketplace, they found there were a lot of nearly numb audiophiles who rejoiced at the break from disco.

Anyone who follows Nick Lowe's recording career knows the man's talent for the catch phrase: His first solo album, released in early 1978, is the now-famous *Jesus of Cool* (U.K.)/*Pure Pop for Now People* (U.S.). On the cover Lowe poses as a "rock star for all people," in Bruce Springsteen/Jackson Browne/Flamin' Groovies fashions. Classic Lowe lines include "I made an American squirm/And it felt so right" and "Girls like that bring a lump to my pocket." While Lowe was instrumental in the rise of the pub-rock movement, an unflagging rallier to ragged rhythm, his reputation in the States came largely from his production of Elvis's albums.

Costello gave flesh to the skeleton, providing a wealth of material to back Riviera's flashy promises and Lowe's commitment to pure pop. Their talents mesh peculiarly: The same issue of *Rolling Stone* that praised *My Aim Is True* panned Graham Parker and the Rumour's *Stick To Me* for Lowe's "muddy production." *My Aim Is True* bears the words that Lowe worked on it for "Keepitasahobby Productions."

Lowe has always been frank about his intentions and long-term expectations from the music industry: "I just want to make a big pile and get out while the going is good," he told *Rolling Stone* in 1978. Yet Lowe, Riviera, and Costello were perhaps more sensitive to "the kids," their record buyers, than their quotes and entanglements with the press indicate, earning Elvis the nickname (no pun intended) of "bonus baby" for his habit of including extras, such as 45s of live versions, postcards, or buttons, with the initial pressings of his albums. One of the real gems produced from this practice was the 45-EP included with Rockpile's *Seconds of Pleasure*, a tribute to the Everly Brothers by Nick Lowe and Dave Edmunds with the two posed on the cover just like Don and Phil, holding what may be the original Everly guitars. Lowe looks like the angel who finally got hold of Elvis's red shoes.

No matter how mired in litigation, intimidated or burned or ignored by the press this group of musicians would become, it seems they never lost their sense of play in the studio. Lowe and Edmunds would drift from group to group, label to label, producing, singing, releasing solo and Rockpile albums, and still be able to do a song like "They Call It Rock," a catalog of the confusion and madness of rockbiz yet performed with the kind of energy that lets you know they'd think of doing nothing else. "Music for Money" ("singing for socks") is along the same lines (both are from *Pure Pop*). As the Ramones would later say, "We're not prisoners of rock and roll. We're volunteers." In March of 1981, Rockpile dissolved, with Dave Edmunds citing irreconcilable differences with Jake Riviera.

My Aim Is True proved that all the hoopla over "Zero" was justified. Listening now, the record seems remarkably tame, with a distinct seventies pop flavor lacing the fifties rock & roll edges. "Watching the Detectives," released on the eve of the Live Stiffs tour and included on the U.S. version of *My Aim Is True* once its popularity in the U.K. became apparent, would later give Elvis his first top-ten single. "Zero" had piqued interest; it had mystified. "Watching the Detectives" riveted. Elvis would later say it was the first song that showed he could try a different style. Its reggae beat and insinuating bass lines were obvious descendants of punk's flirtation with third-world culture, later culminating in the Clash's *Sandinista!* (In fact, he admitted he'd written the song after nonstop replays of the Clash's first album, *London's Burning*.) But Costello shows his real strength in the sense of theater of "Watching the Detectives." Like "Zero" or "Waiting for the End of the World" or "Mystery Dance," it is a little story, a grainy B-movie plot.

"Detectives" showed Costello's best aspects of incorporating the mediocrity of middle-class life as backdrop for seething seediness. The singer and his girl sit watching a detective thriller, she ignoring him, one eye on the set, one eye on her manicure. The cheapness of the movie and the cheapness of their lives soon meld into a twilight-zone scene bathed

59

in blue-gray light. During the course of the song, the singer takes the step from begging for favors from this vacant girlie so enthralled with the "cute" movie to assuming the cold, hair-trigger machismo of a Capone. The desperate turns desperado. Her parents turn up "prepared to hear the worse" now that their daughter has vanished, and the singer gets coy. "It only took my little fingers to blow you away." The cheery organ riffs chill: "Don't get *cute*," Costello threatens.

The rest of *My Aim Is True* shows Elvis at his sweetest: "Miracle Man," "Alison," and "Mystery Dance" all have that heartrending teen-age tragedy about them, at once touching and hilarious. Costello would use the word "dance" again as a euphemism for sex—"No Dancing (When They Get Home)"—but never so close to home as in "Mystery Dance." The singer's desperate confusion and frustration call up all those horrible reminiscences of adolescent urges: burning curiosity and damning guilt, rumors of how to do it and whom to do it to, cheap magazines, backseats, locker rooms...ah, the teen years.

"Less Than Zero" and *My Aim Is True*, along with the hazy bio that went with them, indeed proved irresistible to American rockbiz. The major American mag, *Rolling Stone*, picked up Elvis's trajectory just as *My Aim Is True* shot into the U.K. charts a mere two weeks after its release. The U.S. critics were clearly as eager to embrace the Next Big Thing as their counterparts overseas. At that point, the Sex Pistols's escapades were just beginning to break; it would be another full year before discomania peaked with *Saturday Night Fever*.

Anglophiles who were avid scavengers of the import record bins caught on early, but for the most part, Elvis was lumped with the rest of the ill-fed and ashen lot who had stomped into the consciousness of the masses demanding ATTENTION NOW. The reaction of that venerable king of record buyers, Joe College, was suspicion. Tinkering with his new Dolby cassette unit on the massive stereo crammed into a tiny dorm, he carefully preened his new Eagles album and chuckled amiably at the record companies' new hype. But his reaction would turn from patronizing to confused and at last to horror as the new music took hold. There was a lot of "You call that music?" and "It's just a fad," and "My six-year-old sister could do better than that," which eventually turned to alarmed gasps of "Safety pins! In their noses! Decadence! Deviance! This is not music...this is dangerous!"; and for some the uncanny familiarity of

60

Right: Top of the Pops, 1978.

At top, a Spanish import single; bottom, a German issue.

those parental-sounding phrases was enough to make them shut their mouths and listen.

But, to be fair, the Sex Pistols' sudden seizure of the press was probably the first exposure most Americans had to the movement. American radio stations and record labels were even more notorious for their lily-livered impotence than their U.K. counterparts for ignoring their own burgeoning talents. Tiny pockets of counterculture arose in the most unlikely spots—on the wino-infested Bowery in New York, along the Strip in L.A., in Rubber City Akron, Ohio, and Athens, Georgia; but rarely did Tampa know what Chattanooga was up to. The record industry showed every indication of following the suit of the publishing and film industries: More and more, the medium-sized audience was ignored in favor of making a gamble on the huge profit margin of the next best seller or blockbuster movie. The Next Big Thing. And, in fact, the Sex Pistols *were* a fabrication much like Kiss or Queen or, later, the Plasmatics. To Joe College's great disinterest, he'd heard punk music was born of the "bad conditions" in England. Who wanted to buy the vomit of a dying culture? Disco may have taught him it was fun to dance (having been too young for the great dance music of the early sixties), but anything vaguely resembling a social message was worth rejecting. Until England's second invasion cleared the way for the sublime American mindlessness of "I Wanna Be Sedated" and "Die Young, Stay Pretty," American fans scratched their heads in puzzlement at what sounded like a throwback to political activism. After all, everyone knew the revolution had failed.

So when Elvis first strode into the spotlight, just a lone, angry wimp with an old Fender Jazzmaster, Americans who listened were surprised to hear a literate intelligence behind those anguished screams. Knowledge of the new wave was limited to hazy details concerning razor blades, transvestism, bizarre names, and a mien of uninterrupted belligerence. There were two forays into the United States by punk groups; and while the Sex Pistols's debut in Atlanta attracted much media hyperbole, most kids just shrugged. Jake Riviera was responsible for the first U.S. tour by a punk group when he took the Damned to the West Coast, and a story appearing in the June 1977 *Rolling Stone* encapsulated many of the elements American fans already associated with the movement. A fight had broken out backstage when Joan Jett (then with the Runaways) began playing with the Damned's backstage phone. Drummer Rat Scabies and Brian James then had it out, and the delightful mood of the evening carried over into their performance, which was marked by taunts from the audience. A beer bottle was bounced off Dave Vinian's head. Scabies responded by challenging the offenders to a fight and throwing drumsticks, and soon Riviera joined him, coming onstage to scream at the "bored" Californians with their "fucking Cadillacs." Bassist Captain Sensible took off his nurse's uniform in protest. Fighting carried over into the parking lot that night, and Jake later mused, "I don't know why they fought over Joan in the first place. She fucking doesn't even have big tits."

Meanwhile, record company execs began gnashing their teeth as the Clash and Sid Vicious chipped away at the California sound's hold on the charts.

Even now, Americans will preface a comment about Elvis with, "I don't like punk rock, but I like him." It's hard to believe the tunes sounded so threatening then. Besides the two that received the most airplay, "Watching the Detectives" and "Alison," there are some that sound downright buoyant. "Red Shoes" is one of these, along with "Sneaky Feelings" and "Miracle Man." And then there's that sissy organ, which would seem to defuse whatever real defiance that might come from the songs. When the Attractions materialized behind Elvis to replace Clover, the group on the album, Nieve's purposefully monotonous repetition didn't debunk the myth; it heightened it, giving that dizzying realization that there was something devious lurking behind the lead singer. Pete Thomas's drums also took on some of Costello's character: There are awkward sputterings and stutters, like those that make "Watching the Detectives" so effective.

But to Costello the most important theme of *My Aim Is True* was the focus on the loser, the aspect he contended was something totally new to rock & roll, heretofore limited to country music. Rock & roll is basically a macho form of music, he told Nick Kent of *NME*, and his was the first to describe the status of the complete loser without descending to weepy introspection. "Sneaky Feelings" was another song Costello would point to with pride as lyrically "new"; it deals with the aspects of a relationship one normally tries to hide. Costello later referred to it fondly as a "nasty, greasy little song."

Between the time of the release of Elvis's album and the subsequent furor in the press, Elvis quietly waited. He'd told the press that he knew all along what the reaction to his music would be, and the first line of the first song on *My Aim Is True* bears him out: "Now that your picture's in the paper being rhythmically admired..."

February 1981: English Mugs Tour, New York City's Palladium.

Left: Promo poster for Trust. Opposite: (top) Elvis in foreground, backed by the fabulous Attractions (left to right: Steve Nieve, Bruce Thomas, Pete Thomas) in an early photo. (below) Britannia rules the new wave... Elvis as he appeared in the movie Americathon.

"Talking in the Dark/Wednesday Week" give-away single from Elvis' marathon weekend in New York, Spring '79.

Elvis and Glen whisper and scream. New York City, February '81.

A reference to Elvis' favorite movie.

At the same time, he was also prepared for the fickle public. Not that he catered to it the way Kiss or Queen had with glitter rock, for example, but in the same way the greats (Presley, Holly, the Beatles) had. He virtually invented himself. He was a songwriter who came with a ready-made legend—Local Dork Makes Good. And he came prepared to exploit the exploitation. In July of 1977 the Sex Pistols were still the hottest "media event" in the U.K., their single "God Save the Queen" still high on the charts, "Pretty Vacant" just released, their film in the making, their picture on the covers of every major music mag in the U.K. Costello's pose as the modern bad boy may have been a joke in England, but that was to be Columbia's promo angle in America. He was only too willing to comply. There appeared to be a hole that was just Elvis-sized: he was the punk who'd been pushed around too long, yes, but he didn't seem the type to kick you with his jackboots. He'd be more apt to delay your application for an auto loan.

Even an event that could have been disastrous to Costello's career proved perversely beneficial: The more corpulent Elvis died just as Costello was launching his media blitz. The ambiguous "Elvis is King" promos for *My Aim Is True* were quietly dropped. Ironically, Costello's first big interview, with Nick Kent of *NME*, England's highly revered music rag, landed in the same issue commemorating Presley's death at Graceland. Elvis is dead—long live Elvis. The title: "D. P. Costello, of Whitton, Middlesex, It Is Your Turn to Be The Future of Rock & Roll."

There are perhaps a couple of reasons why Costello granted Kent an interview. Kent is apparently something of a local celebrity in his own right (among his credits is a short stint as a member of the Sex Pistols), and frequent references to his Keith Richard, leather-clad persona appear in *NME*'s letters and columns. Costello had seen him on at least two occasions: once when Kent was covering another group at the Marquee, a local club, and patently ignoring Costello (Kent barely escaped "the list" on that occasion); and another time on a tube bound for Osterley. Costello was so struck with the image of the writer stumbling onto the train, oblivious to the other passengers' perturbation, that he drew on the incident for the song "Waiting for the End of the World." He told Kent he was the guy in the opening verse.

Also, the interview took place in a bar; and while Kent and Costello talked, a woman from Island Records (Warner Brothers in the U.S.) seated herself at the table. Since Island Records execs appeared prominently in "the list" for spurning him early in his career, this was not a wise or healthy move. Costello savored rejecting her, and he and Kent drew closer, like co-conspirators. They talked for four hours. Kent called him "El."

That interview would be the most substantial until Mick Brown of *The Times* was permitted to follow him on tour. Costello appears in his most natural state: coiled. He describes the new version of "Less Than Zero" he'll write for the States. He talks about his religious background, his boyhood in Liverpool (perhaps the only town he likes), music, but not about his wife and son—he says he's "very country music" about his private life. It is in this interview that he says his motivation for writing is "revenge and guilt," which will spread like plague through the rest of the articles about Costello for months to come. He reveals that *GP* is his favorite album and that he wants to die young. Like Gram Parsons. Kent asks him if he's looking forward to a drug death in a sleazy motel. Costello allows he saw it "more like being run over by a bus."

Perhaps what Costello didn't expect was that Kent would find out about Costello's early bluegrass days, his job at Elizabeth Arden, his hometown, or that Lowe and Riviera thought him talented but "a bit loopy."

And although Costello vehemently denied he wanted to go to America (just as the Sex Pistols did—to the delight of English fans), he would begin a U.S. tour in the fall. Obviously, America has too great a market to ignore, but Costello retained the attitude that put him where he is today: Bite the big one, trendies.

And so it was that Elvis Costello elected to move into the circus arena of rock culture. Hurried plans were made for a fourteen-city itinerary, beginning November 16 at San Francisco's Old Waldorf. The fact that Clover, the backup group on *My Aim Is True*, had originally come from there couldn't have hurt; area record stores were having trouble keeping up with the demands of the greedy public. FM stations picked up the interest and "Red Shoes," "Alison," and "Watching the Detectives" wafted over U.S. airwaves. KSAN, the area's leading FM station, interviewed him, and Costello told him his name really was Elvis and, once again, that his organ player had never heard "? and the Mysterians". The rock press was poised, and his fans at home waited breathlessly for news of Elvis's adventures in McDonaldland. He showed up at the punk hideaway Mabuhay Gardens to see another raspy-voiced singer-songwriter, Randy Newman, whose album, *Little Criminals*, had just been released. He remained unimpressed.

The first reviews by the industry rags that had so greedily consumed the Pistols' exploits were more standoffish towards Elvis, submitting him, to a much closer scrutiny. Greil Marcus, in a review for *Rolling Stone* titled "Elvis: His Aim Is Off," wondered about the "autohype" involved. Apparently, the combination of the Attractions's mod clothes and "Batman-theme" sound was for him, a bit weak. Simon Frith's lengthy musing in the *Village Voice* tried to place Costello's source of anger and pointed to the lyrics of "Less Than Zero": "Rather than being annoyed by the specific lies of fascists, Costello is taken with the insidious notion that nothing matters." It should be noted that while Frith is English, the two reviews are typical of the deadly serious examination American reviewers sometimes place on popular music.

But American audiences were every bit as wild for him as in the U.K., and across the country, his appearance would be marked as *the* rock event of the year.

American rock fans were greatly impressed, but also a little amused.

And intimidated—the campaign was working. Somewhere over the Atlantic, Elvis had taken on greater stature as a threatening eminence. In Britain writers had commented more on the twerpy computer-operator appearance, and more than one over here noted the Woody Allen–Buddy Holly touches. It was rumored that his glasses were props. But Costello came on so thoroughly confident, so insistent in his demand for attention, laughter died in the throats of the most cynical of the ink-stained wretches. Once he got your attention, he had the skill to hold it. And once he had you enthralled, he stalked away pouting. In America, his roots were even more clouded in enigma—he told the press pretty much what he chose, and soon fans had another hero. He even made *Time* magazine and in '78 told *Newsweek*, "I'm here to corrupt America's youth. But my visa will probably run out before I have a chance to do it."

His shows were marked by his manic style: tension pitched to such a fever that his skinny body twitched as if possessed by demons. He grasped the mike stand with arms and knees—a male equivalent of Marilyn Monroe housed in the body of Mr. Peepers—spat, grimaced, and barely contained his malevolence to the framework of his songs. Yet he'd expressed surprise to *NME* that the album had been described in terms of paranoia and sadomasochism. He'd felt most were tender songs about losing. Whether he'd decided to give the crowds what he thought they wanted (or deserved) or that this was the absolutely furious young man for a dying decade was unclear. At the Whisky in West Hollywood, a heckler began shouting. Costello threw a drink in his face and then wielded the broken drinking glass to show he meant business. "*One of these days, I'm going to pay it back...*" Later, in July of 1978, bass player Bruce Thomas was reported to have received eighteen stitches in the hand after trying to demonstrate the correct "barroom method" of breaking a beer bottle. (Elvis dedicated "Accidents Will Happen" to him at his London Roundhouse gig, from which the bootleg *Accidents* was taped.)

Along the way, amid the ballyhoo, he divested himself of the pre-conceptions he'd arrived with. Mostly, he was shocked by the sameness of it, especially after seeing Detroit (Motown!) was "just another city." Of all the cities, he liked Chicago best. "People were rude, you know?" What a great city for Costello—the scene of so many B movies...corrupt politicians...gangsters...*detectives!* The bill was also a killer—the opening act was Tom Petty and the Heartbreakers at the Riviera Theater,

69

Left: "Woody Allen sings Nietzsche..."

at the bargain-basement price of three dollars. Petty, et al. had just released "American Girl" and were finally seeing a little promise of recognition after years of near obscurity. Petty is another who benefited from the moods of moderns, his albums languishing in the cut-rate bins in record stores until black leather came back in style. They agreed to the price in hopes of expanding their audience, and the 1800-seat theater was filled to capacity. A veritable "Star Wars."

Al Rudis of the *Chicago Sun-Times* was impressed with TPH but didn't quite know what to do with Costello's "hard and nasty" music. "It would be freak rock if not for the songs and real talent of the band, but both are masterful..." he said and finally decided that the impression of disorientation the group made was, in the end, the real excitement of the set.

Philadelphia's Hot Club next provided 600 zealots who screamed, pulled their hair, and worked themselves into a state of distraction, much to the delight of the *Washington Post*'s music writer, who described the boy wonder after the show sitting quietly on a sofa, staring at his shoes, getting up only to ask for orange juice from the bar while the Attractions gave in to gleeful abandon. Someone asked him if he was excited by all the attention. Elvis shrugged.

In an unusually frank review of *My Aim Is True*, Joseph Sasfy of the *Washington Post* reflected most fans' confusion about Elvis's music: "The truth is, I don't know what many of these songs are about. Like Dylan's best, I'm living on lyrical snatches that grow in meaning in relation to everything that is misunderstood."

Finally, Elvis brought Alison and the detectives and his red shoes to New York, and the result was a small feast in the press, whetted in part by the bait Elvis had set in omnipotent *Time* magazine, thoroughly trashing his own country and then turning on the States with an even more vitriolic attack. Among the more memorable Costello diagnoses: The British are "stupid" for retaining the monarchy, American punks are "just rich hippies whining about the Vietnam war," and a description of the apparent satisfaction of the English with their mediocre lives and the converse American waste of their material wealth. The motives of "Mr. Costello" were again questioned, this time by John Rockwell in *The New York Times*, who wrote that the menacing stage presence seemed "as distracting and irrelevant as Leo Sayer's mime-white face." Rockwell, suggesting Costello might jettison this visual baggage, says, "While he's at it, he might get a sharper band..." but does describe the performance as "interesting, satisfying." On the other hand, the *New York Post*, that hysterical chronicler of urban cataclysm, loved him, comparing him to "the kid who might just show up on the doorstep of Sun Records to cut some discs."

The New York–based television program "Saturday Night Live" was at that time beginning to attract a healthy number of viewers for its late-night doses of satire, absurdity, and music. In weeks past producer Lorne Michaels had appeared on the show, suavely confident he could lure the Beatles into their studios for a reunion. He was prepared to offer them, he said, "Five hundred dollars. That's right, *five hundred* dollars.... You can split it up any way you like.... Give Ringo a little less...."This having failed, behind-the-scenes negotiations began to bring the Sex Pistols into American living rooms. At the same time, "SNL" started its "Anyone Can Host" contest, inviting viewers to send in postcards stating in twenty-five words or less why they should host the show. Alas, the Sex Pistols's manager, Malcolm MacLaren, backed down at the last minute; and Michaels expressed regret that the winner of the contest, an eighty-eight-year-old grandmother, did not get to introduce the band; but she did hesitatingly pronounce the name "...Elvis Costello?". He, in stifling tweeds, and the Attractions, a motley-looking group with their paisleys and granny glasses (one sporting a "Thanks, Malc" T-shirt), graced the screen for the first time. Costello leaned into the mike, leered into the camera, and "Watching the Detectives" snaked into the homes of the nation's insomniacs. They began the familiar iambs of "Less Than Zero" for their second number, but Costello dramatically cut them off after the opening bars to choose a more appropriate selection. He then sneered "Radio, Radio" coast to coast. In back of the cameras, the technical crew was less than pleased with this sudden turn of events. The feedback hadn't died from the mikes before the band slammed down their equipment and stormed off. The "SNL" crew told them, according to Costello, that they wouldn't be invited back. ("Evidently, it's not *that* live," he would say later.) But American fans had their first real glimpse of Britain's latest export.

The first tour ended in Asbury Park, New Jersey. (An ironic point of exit—last year's model Bruce Springsteen was at home there, recovering from acute overexposure due to simultaneous *Time* and *Newsweek* cover stories in 1976. Elvis had confided to Kent that he thought Springsteen "a lousy lyricist." However, he may have changed his

The Swedish cover for This Year's Model *is an oddly flat picture of a picture.*

opinion—*Rolling Stone* reported seeing him backstage at Springsteen's recent London gig.) Elvis would tour the United States three times in the twelve months following his debut in San Francisco.

Plans for the next tour were already under way—by February he would begin another, far more extensive and grueling foray into the hinterlands and soft underbelly of suburban life, with one-night stands stretching across the continent from late March to the end of June. In April Nick Lowe and Dave Edmunds joined the tour, along with Mink DeVille, replacing Willy Alexander and the Boom Boom Band. Also in the spring Elton John won Britain's Capital Radio Award for the Best Male Singer of 1977. He thanked the crowd but told them Elvis really deserved the award. "He is the greatest rock singer in Britain today."

This Year's Model: The title put the finger squarely on Costello's predicament. Fully aware of his "media baby" boom, he lampooned the trend while profiting from it, but also suffered from the potentially humiliating combination of Knowing and Being. The term "poseur" had already cropped up, and it was the most-feared label of the new-music tribe. The only escape from it seemed to be martyrdom, and Costello in his early career, like Sid Vicious, said he fervently hoped to die young.

The first two albums have an eerie quality of what Costello would realize was a "self-fulfilling prophecy." Jeering at trendiness, he'd become the new trend.

Riviera showed his skill again at designing ads: Elvis peered out from behind his camera in full-page ads in rock weeklies: "Elvis Costello: Is he on your list? ARE YOU ON HIS?"

This Year's Model shows a good deal of change from *My Aim Is True*, with more complex, more menacing lyrics and a sound that comes off less a hybrid of Chuck Berry and Lou Reed than something original, a group rather than a singer and backup. Originally named *Little Hitler*, the album's title was changed after Nick Lowe borrowed the name for a song of his own. Elvis struck back by penning "Two Little Hitlers." The concentration on trendyism is ever-present ("This Year's Girl" "The Beat," "Radio, Radio"), and Costello states his aim to stay away from "Chelsea" —his term for the epitome of the new in-crowd. ("(I Don't Want to Go to) Chelsea" and "Night Rally" were omitted from the American version.) But there's still the same old Elvis, awkward and fumbling in "Pump It Up," a "Subterranean Homesick Blues"–like chant. Costello takes his cue from the new fall TV season: There's more violence, more raw sex, but he is at a complete loss when it comes to simple touching.

With *This Year's Model* came renewed charges of misogyny, and Costello bristled, saying the reasoning behind the songs was just the opposite. "This Year's Girl," he claimed, was the flip side of "Miracle Man," and both were satirical songs about inadequacy.

The Mick Brown interview for London's *Sunday Times* in the summer of 1978 was the most intimate look at Costello yet. He was on the road, ready to open his third tour in California, staying in the Tropicana Motel in Los Angeles, in the very same room where Sam Cooke met his inglorious end.

The hype increased: A huge billboard of Elvis behind his *This Year's Model* camera loomed over Sunset Boulevard. The Whiskey-A-Go-Go served an "Elvis Costello Special"—fish and chips—and a record store ran an Elvis Costello look-alike contest. Riviera vetoed an idea from Columbia for eyeglass-frame giveaways with the album. Elvis arrived poolside dressed in full, ill-fitting suit and shirt buttoned tight to talk about life in what he called "The Promised Land." He seemed relaxed in the presence of a fellow countryman, and was frank, funny, and, well, charming. America, he said, is either "dazzling or mundane"; what was more interesting to him was the middle ground in England: "that seething sort of atmosphere in which nothing ever goes out of control... the underachieving the society is based on."

From snatches of news releases across the country and in the U.K., a composite forms. Concert halls are turned into veritable battlefields and fans are pulled into the camps of Lowe, Costello, or DeVille, depending on their preferences. We see a few glimpses of Costello after the shows, drinking, sometimes friendly, sometimes funny, but more often completely inaccessible.

In a story titled "DeVille Outguns Costello in New Wave Showdown," the Orpheum concert in Boston is described. There's no sign in the press of any tension among the groups, but it must be high. The same article quotes Willy DeVille as saying, "I can dance and he can't. I've got it all over him in street moves." His friends and his record company all say the same thing: "Bury him. Put him away." (In the *Wet* interview, Costello retorted, "Willy DeVille's a jerk.") While Costello was on, a woman in the front had an epileptic seizure—Costello went forward on bended knee to see that she was helped and soothe the uneasiness at the spot. In Austin's Municipal Auditorium, he spotted the rent-a-cops pushing kids back into their seats. "It's a fucking prison camp here," he raged and burst into "This Year's Girl." The *Austin American-Statesman*'s Bob Claypool complained, "Costello can spit out venom with the best of them, BUT I've already got enough of my own, see?" Several theaters they played were less than packed—there were 900 fans and 3,300 empty seats in Tampa—but Costello seems to have threatened everyone with the same words: "Tell your friends about us, because when we come back I want to see this place *full*."

In Dallas Costello took a break to see Delbert McClinton at a local hillbilly roadhouse and even joined him onstage for a couple of songs. Afterward he stayed at the bar for several hours, talking with friends and drinking Lone Star beer. He told writer Pete Oppel that he's not "mad at the world" as many think; he'd been considering an album of "more subdued material." He told him about finding a much-sought-after Kenny and the Casuals record, about the simple lighting techniques of his show, and his lighting man, who he said was actually a designer of heaters.

"Sometimes I feel like I'm standing in front of a heater when I'm on that stage." And about Kansas City: "You can get fat before you can get drunk."

Among the albums giving live versions of Costello sets is *Live at the El Macambo*, recorded for CBS Canada for radio airplay with a pressing of 500, and the bootleg of this album, an almost exact replica. *Exit* is another, a bootleg compilation of 1977 and 1978 shows. Both reveal Elvis and the Attractions in top form, racing through the sets, egging the fans on ("These guys have the right idea—they're standing *oop.*"), and generally knocking 'em dead. And refusing encores.

Live at the El Mocambo (Toronto, March 6, 1978), shows a more talkative Elvis than earlier reports describe. He prods the crowd, teases them with snatches of improvisation, and tells them he's glad to be back in a club after playing in front of all those dull American students. He tells them he's come from England to take the country back. The local news

75

Above: A face in the crowd.

clipping reprinted on the back is titled "Prince Charmless Fashions Event."

Martin Belmont of Rumour accompanied them, as he would on later tours. Elvis played them the Dallas version of "Less Than Zero."

Costello wrote the Dallas version after finding out that American listeners, hearing the words "Oswald," "Turn up the TV," and "home movies" naturally thought the song referred to Lee Harvey and the first installment in what would become an increasingly familiar routine for Americans: the lone gunman, the sudden tragedy, the hours of near-hysterical coverage by anxious reporters. The new verses fit quite well into the song's deadly cynical reprise ("Everything means less than zero") and suggest an equally grisly, perverted scenario as Oswald's mutilation and bedding of the boy vandal in the U.K. version. However, Costello, possibly disconcerted by the slightly morbid response from American fans, suddenly dropped the song from the group's repertoire, refusing repeated requests for it from American fans who had perhaps seen the Zapruder film rerun just once too often.

Whatever Costello may have had in mind for that album of "more mellow songs," *This Year's Model* certainly isn't it. Most of the songs are relentless, aggressive syncopations: "The Beat," "Pump It Up," "You Belong to Me," "Hand in Hand," "Lip Service," "Lipstick Vogue," and "Radio, Radio," which set some to wondering—if the song was successful, it would alienate disc jockeys, press agents, and the media in general. But if it were successful in a monetary sense, it would force them to welcome Costello into their enclave to become another extension of their marketing schemes and recipient at awards dinners. A writer for *Rolling Stone* said: "I predict an empty chair."

In September Costello performed at the Rock Against Racism rally in Brockwell Park, Brixton, and went to work in Holland on his new album, tentatively titled *Emotional Fascism*. And made plans to tour the United States again.

I Stand Accused

A little over a year had passed since Costello was arrested in front of the London Hilton. After spending a month sequestered in a recording studio (A month! Rockbiz marveled), Costello was readying the album, whose name he had changed from *Emotional Facism* to the less drastic *Armed Forces*, for the marketplace. At about the same time, reports of Elvis squiring model Bebe Buell around appeared in print. *NME*'s end-of-the-year "T-Zers Awards" included one "Tammy Wynette D.I.V.O.R.C.E Award to Elvis Costello." The link between the gangly singer and svelte Buell, whom Random Notes tactfully described as a "seasoned rock star companion," left many fans aghast. She seemed the living portrait of what Elvis (our Elvis!) would hate. Her name had been associated with a long line of performers, the most recent being Rod Stewart; she seemed trenchantly trendy. But she was a mere foreshadowing of the trouble the initials BB would bring in the months to come.

In September of 1978 Costello appeared in Brixton's Brockwell Park at one of England's own brand of "happenings." Rock Against Racism (RAR) was throwing its Carnival 2. Their bills were virtual explosions of the best new talent around: the Clash, Gang of Four, Tom Robinson, X-Ray Specs, Steel Pulse, and Stiff Little Fingers had all played RAR events.

Born of fans' disgust at racist comments Eric Clapton made at a concert in August of 1976, RAR had hosted the groups with the assistance of

other organizations, such as Rock Against Sexism, Vegetarians Against Nazis, the Legalize Cannabis movement, and Skateboarders Against Racism. Clapton had used the time between his sets to inform the crowd that Britain was in danger of becoming a colony because of the horde of "foreigners" descending on its shores; he also urged the election of Enoch Powell, an archconservative known for supporting legislation restricting immigration. He had touched a sensitive nerve. A letter signed by several attending the concert appeared in *Melody Maker* a few weeks later. "We nearly puked," they wrote. "Own up, Eric. Half your music is black. Where would you be without blues and R&B?" (Clapton later apologized.) They stated their intention to form a group to fight "the racial poison in rock music," and Rock Against Racism was begun.

Far from spouting the preachy didacticism their name might imply, RAR simply aims to present a balance of black, white, and Asian music, a mixture of cultures. This mix, however, is not without potential danger; RAR combines groups that attract both Pakistanis and Paki bashers (gangs who roam England's streets beating Asians for kicks). A typical RAR rally might include Sham '69, a "skinhead" group, insuring the attendance of the skinhead-suedehead gangs (who are often described as National Front sympathizers), and Steel Pulse, a reggae group, thus guaranteeing the Rastamen will also show. Said one of the RAR founders: "If a skinhead kid swings his ass to black music, at least he's got a contradiction to go home with." So far, the RAR rallies have been remarkably peaceful. Their offices, however, have twice been set afire. (RAR has released an album, *RAR'S Greatest Hits,* including studio cuts from the Clash, Tom Robinson, Mekons, Sham '69, and Costello. See Discography.)

Six months later RAR's New York chapter would send pickets to Costello's shows.

Late fall and early spring of 1978–79 seemed full of evil portents. In October Sid Vicious of the Sex Pistols was arrested in New York for the murder of his girlfriend, Nancy Spungeon, at the Chelsea Hotel, and the potential of another British Invasion crumbled into disarray. The group had disbanded in San Francisco after a resounding "So what?" reception across the country. Malcolm McLaren, ever poised, suggested the group might now reunite to help Sid with medical and legal fees (F. Lee Bailey was to defend Vicious), and in his London King's Road shop McLaren featured a thirteen-dollar T-shirt showing Sid surrounded by dead roses with the logo "I'M ALIVE, SHE'S DEAD, I'M YOURS."

By February, when Costello and the Attractions opened at the Long Beach Arena on yet another U.S. tour, Vicious, too, would be dead from an overdose of heroin after a party celebrating his release on bail. The event completed the short-circuit success of the Sex Pistols, and as *Trouser Press* editor Ira A. Robbins said, "The new wave had reached its Altamont."

Meanwhile, Costello seemed eager to make up to England the time he'd spent in the States. He blitzed the countryside, touring with Richard Hell and the Voidoids and John Cooper Clarke, and presided over a seven-day, sellout stayover at London's Dominion Theatre. Rockpile was off doing their good deed, performing at a benefit concert with the Damned, Tyla Gang and Dr. Feelgood for French promoter Marc Zermati, who claimed his recent drug bust was a frame.

Armed Forces was released, after a short delay, in the first week of January. By far more complex than *My Aim Is True* and *This Year's Model,* the album showed Costello had honed his most arresting array of images. Departing from the vignettes and teen anger of the two previous albums, *Armed Forces* was a variation on the theme of the military strategics of romance, with Costello as toy-room soldier. The British version featured a perforated set of postcards of tanks and soldiers folding in to form the gatefold cover, and the back displayed a bull elephant leading a herd in a charge. (Odd Trivia Note: When the B-52's were forming across the Atlantic in 1977, they briefly considered calling themselves "The Attack Elephants.") Under the postcards was the same Jackson Pollock–style drip graphic that U.S. fans knew.

The sleeve retains the name that Costello reportedly changed at the last minute—*Emotional Facism.* There's a marvelous picture inside, showing Elvis draped over the diving board of a lush Palm Springs pool, his hands dangling from the sleeves of another suit of drab, thick cloth. His white socks glaring in the sunlight, he is a splotch of dread intruding Eden's calm.

The lyrics were also the most controversial—several songs had a decidedly political bent. "Oliver's Army," written after a visit to Northern Ireland, has a bright, merry organ riff but paints a bleak picture of Britain after the Empire ("We could send you to Johannesburg"). There are more

London's Dominion, Tottenham Court Road, 1978.

twists and surprises—"Hand In Hand" and "You Belong to Me" are not love songs of the Carly Simon genre but denials: "(I don't want anybody saying) You Belong to Me." There are Beatles lines ("Time is running out..."), and classic pop riffs throughout, reminiscent of *Abbey Road*. But Costello always manages to provide his own perspective. "Green Shirt" is about Angela Rippon (the British version of Barbara Walters), with whom the singer has a running dialogue. "Accidents Will Happen" rates with "Watching the Detectives" for eeriness but has its own degree of earnestness ("It's the damage that we do/And never know/It's the words that we don't say/That scare me so"). The relationship as hit and run.

A facist/victim theme runs throughout, but it's hard to tell whether the target is politics, love, or rockbiz. "White niggers," from "Oliver's Army," and "You'll never make a lampshade out of me," from "Goon Squad," are a couple of examples.

Included with the first 10–50,000 pressings of the album was a 7-inch live version of "Watching the Detectives," "Accidents Will Happen," and "Alison," recorded at the Hollywood High concert, where Linda Ronstadt first heard Elvis and decided on her own phrasing for the song. She recorded it for her *Living in the USA* album. "How Do I Make You," which also became a hit for Ronstadt, was one of several on *Mad Love* written by Mark Goldenburg of the Cretones and was a decided departure from her MOR-California Sound-bluegrass manifestations of the past. Waves of disgust emanated from Elvis's camp at the sound of Ronstadt's velvet tones crooning "Alison."

The American tour would begin in February, and various Stiff alumni, like Rockpile, the Damned, and Clover (this time backing Carlene Carter), would also appear on these shores. Again Elvis would first materialize on the West Coast and work his own Manifest Destiny eastward. And again Riviera would show his own inimitable style in promotions. Roadies were outfitted in green fatigues and the silver touring bus's destination sign would read "Camp LeJeune, N.C." Full-page ads included one of Elvis holding a minibazooka to his mouth with the headline "PAY ATTENTION" above and, beside the pinless grenade to his right, "BE MERCENARY. GET ARMED FORCES."

Costello and the Attractions opened their tour with the Rubinoos, veterans of the Berserkely label, whose act showcased such bits of sixties rock fluff as "Sugar, Sugar" and other saccharine-y covers, but some members of the press were impressed with their freshness and appeal.

However, the Berkeley crowd was not prepared to warmly welcome their native sons; the group was booed thoroughly. Some of their set went unheard, because of the incessant chants of "Elvis! Elvis!" Costello, in a silver lame jacket and baggy checked pants, made his usual impressive showing at the Long Beach Arena, and although for the most part writers chorused the familiar praise, a few, after the Sex Pistols debacle, turned warily to the lyrics of *Armed Forces* and speculated that Costello might be another capitalizing on our collective guilt. The word *poseur* flecked a few articles. *Armed Forces,* though, proved popular: Along with Blondie's *Parallel Lines,* it would become the first so-called new wave album to achieve gold status in spite of the overwhelming popularity of disco. At the time, the Bee Gees were nearly ubiquitous; their white-suited figures peered out from covers of *Rolling Stone, Newsweek, Crawdaddy,* and even the ultraconservative high-finance chronicle *Fortune.*

The band went on to Santa Barbara and San Diego, but when they hit Seattle, trouble again arose. "ELVIS LAID AN EGG" was the local headline; his set was cut from the usual hour to forty minutes, and that was where fans drew the line. Outraged, they stamped, bleated, screamed, but to no avail. Someone onstage finally produced a piercing feedback signal from the amps, which very effectively cleaned out the hall. Still angry, some set fire to concert posters on their way out. Carlene Carter also appeared in February, at L.A.'s Palomino, a country show-case, backed by the ever present Clover. Costello, too, played the Palomino, accompanied by Clover's steel guitarist John McFee, resulting in the inevitable bootleg, *Live at the Palomino.* "Somebody probably thought we were a western swing band," Elvis joked, this time sporting a black-and-white houndstooth-checked jacket, black shirt, and snake-thin pink tie. The set included the Fifties theme "Psycho" and the countrified "He'll Have to Go." *Armed Forces* was by this time already in the top fifteen.

Elvis's streak of bad luck continued with the onset of the Grammys, the United States' most prestigious music award. Along with the Cars and Taste of Honey, Costello was nominated for "Best New Artist of the Year." But a look at the Grammy's past recipients—Debby Boone, the Carpenters, even the Swingle Singles (1963)—told the story. Multiple winners that evening were Billy Joel, the Bee Gees, Anne Murray, and Barry Manilow. Artists who came from overseas to attend the ceremony to see their idols in contemporary music were shocked: Bo Diddley wasn't even invited. No one here was very surprised when angry young Elvis lost to Taste of Honey's mindless happy tune "Boogie Oogie Oogie." Perhaps least of all Elvis—who spent the evening at the offices of Andrew Scott and Malcolm Leo, producers of the two-hour "Heroes of Rock & Roll" special (with a title Elvis told Tom Snyder was "a contradiction in terms") that had aired February 9. Elvis was one of the two new artists—along with Bruce Springsteen—to be featured. The show contained rare footage of some never-before-seen films of the early days of Presley and the Beatles, among others; and Costello and the Attractions spent over two hours looking at Presley's Dorsey shows, Chuck Berry, Bob Dylan, and Frankie Lymon. "He loved it," said Scott. Costello and the Attractions appeared in the show in their "Pump It Up" video.

For Valentine's Day he'd treated concert goers at the Palomino to yet another giveaway—this time a version of the classic "My Funny Valentine" on red vinyl, of course. The band added Steve Nieve's song "Sad About Girls" to their repertoire.

But in March they faced a seemingly endless string of one-night stands through the rural plains, farming and dairy communities of the midwestern United States. They entertained themselves as best they could, drinking, watching taped movies on the tour bus' video monitors, going to concerts when they had a chance; and Nieve added another alias ("Steve Adore") to his growing list.

About 3,000 St. Louis concert goers at the Kiel Opera House were witnesses to another sort of Costello tantrum. St. Louis's main FM station, KSHE, had been chosen as the unofficial concert sponsor by Columbia, but apparently someone had bent Elvis's ear with the report that the rival station, KADI, played Armed Forces far more often. He sent his first encore to "all the boys at radio station KADI." Later, the venomous "Radio, Radio" went to "all the local bastard radio stations that don't play our songs...and to KSHE!" The result was a clearly audible thud as Armed Forces was dropped from KSHE's playlist. The album returned to its "heavy rotation" schedule on the station after tour manager Alan Frey called to straighten things out.

The string of one-night stands yawned before them—Dayton, Columbus, Cleveland, Harrisburg, Syracuse, Rochester. Along the way, he tantalized local writers by alternating between Mr. Nice Guy and Martin Bormann poses. Some noticed he was more apt to yell "Thank you" to the audience rather than tersely announcing song titles, as he had done the

previous fall. In Dayton he emphatically told reporter Hal Lipper he was a "songwriter and a singer"—*no* hyphen. When Kent had asked about his motives, Costello answered, "I could never imagine people wanting this ugly geek ramming his songs down people's throats.... I'm in it to disrupt people's lives." A few days later he would do a very good job of that.

It would be another month before the tour would end. Then on the night of March 16, in the aptly low-rent setting of the bar at Columbus's Holiday Inn, Costello delivered the *coup de grace*, alienating both ardent fans and people who had never before heard of him.

The story varies slightly in accounts from several sources, but reactions here and in England were split as wide as the Atlantic.

What is clear from piecing together the various sources is that Stephen Stills and entourage, including back up singer Bonnie Bramlett, percus-

86

sionist Jim Lala, and band manager Jim Lindersmith, had finished their gig in another part of town and were relaxing in the lounge when they spotted Costello and bass player Bruce Thomas and invited the two to join them. They pushed some tables together, and soon the two groups were noisily partying and talking. The trouble began when a local Costello fan began questioning his hero, and soon Costello had launched an attack on American manners and morals (a favorite topic since the *Time* and *Newsweek* interviews). "We hate you," he said. "We just come here for the money." "We're the original white boys, and you're the colonials" was another gem. The report begins to vacillate here—one source states that when Elvis called Americans "just a bunch of flea-bitten greasers and niggers," one of Stills's roadies jerked him up by the collar and told him to shut up. *Rolling Stone's* Random Notes says it was after Elvis called Lala "a greaser spic" that Stills himself did the hoisting, then left the bar in disgust. Bruce Thomas, according to the English sources, tossed "Fuck off, Steel Nose, " after him.

Bramlett, however, stayed on. At thirty-four she was an East St. Louis–born white woman who had come up the hard way, as an Ikette in the Turner Revue, half of Delaney and Bonnie before her marriage split, and back up singer for the cream of the contemporary blues crop: Dickey Betts, Duane Allman, Leon Russell, and Rita Coolidge, among others. She'd just begun to put her life back together after battling alcoholism and slimming down from 180 pounds to 120. She and Stills had returned to the U.S. after playing the Havana Jam two months earlier.

Another admirer asked what Costello thought of Buddy Holly and was answered with an obscenity. "Elvis Presley?" More of the same. (Here, again, the story varies slightly—the English version says the Americans accused Elvis of "stealing" his licks from James Brown, Ray Charles, et. al.) Bramlett had opened the conversation by telling him she admired his music, but when she asked what he thought of James Brown, Costello snapped, "A jive-ass nigger." Bramlett still maintained her temper until she asked, "All right, you son of a bitch, what do you think of Ray Charles?" "He's nothing but an ignorant, blind nigger," quoth Elvis; and when Bramlett suggested he keep his opinions to himself, he said, "Fuck Ray Charles, fuck niggers, and fuck you!" That was enough—Bramlett slapped him hard enough to knock off his glasses. "Don't put the tongue on Ray Charles," she said. Again the account varies: One report has Elvis falling to the floor in the ensuing scuffle, another has him recovering enough to call her a slut, and yet another recounts that one of Stills's roadies hit him hard, knocking him to the floor, and the two bands went at it. "I told him anybody that mean and hateful has to have a little bitty dick," Bramlett said later.

Eddie, the bartender, a small man of Japanese ancestry, went to work, walking straight into the fracas with a nightstick, and later claiming it was really no problem, "just a lot of shoving." Stills's group was dispatched to their waiting bus, and the English faction went upstairs to their rooms.

The story didn't break for a few days, and in the meantime, Elvis was observed here and there wearing an arm sling, apparently from a dislocated shoulder, telling fans at a Nicolette Larson concert in Cleveland that Bonnie Bramlett had taken a swing at him and he fell in the scuffle. However, he recovered in time for his own show at the Cleveland Agora, drawing rave reviews and two encores.

In New York City, meanwhile, mysterious signs materialized: "Where will you be on Elvis Costello weekend?" Below Elvis's pic was "March 31: The Palladium. April 1: Nowhere."

But by the time Elvis was gearing up for the Riviera-inspired "April Fool's Day Marathon"—five gigs in two days in New York—the *Village Voice* (April 2) had broken the story, followed by longer coverage in *Rolling Stone,* most local papers, and a breathy account in the gossip ragsheet *People.* So the Garbo of the rock world was forced to call in his self-proclaimed adversaries—journalists—to give his side of the story. The confrontation occurred on the fourteenth floor of the monolithic CBS building, and industry writers Robert Christgau of the *Voice,* and Chet Flippo and Fred Schruers of *Rolling Stone* were the most visible and vocal fixtures attending. Elvis appeared, slightly shaky, in a polka-dot suit and tie and a small, green lapel button ("Desire Me"). Costello took the you-may-be-wondering-why-I've-called-you-here, take-charge stance and said he wished to make just one statement: "I am not a racist." This may not have been the best comment to offer to a group who still had "I am not a crook" ringing in their ears.

Complaining he'd been "misquoted out of context," Costello explained he'd made the comments in an effort to get rid of the Stills entourage, trying to "outrage these people with ... the most obnoxious and offensive remarks that I could muster. It worked pretty good." He wanted to make clear that the remarks did not represent his actual view.

88

Right: One of the posters that mysteriously materialized on the eve of the marathon weekend in New York.

89

The reporters' reactions ranged from amusement to disbelief to anger. Someone asked why he didn't leave. *"They* didn't..." Someone else asked why the statements were restricted to black performers. Costello replied that the things he'd said about Crosby, Stills, Nash and Young didn't make the press, nor did Bramlett's view that all limeys were "lousy fucks and couldn't get it up anymore." A laugh from the press corps.

He also apologized to Brown and Charles, but more than one writer noted Elvis's adherence to his "don't-ask-me-to-apologize" image. The *Voice's* Richard Goldstein blurted, "You made yourself unavailable... You can't blame it on the press...It was *you!*" One comment seemed to be the most illuminating to Schruers—that everyone had occasion to go to extremes. "Ask Lenny Bruce," said Elvis. But at the end of the conference, it seemed there were more questions than answers.

Fans who had already spent hours deciphering the verses of "Goon Squad" and "Oliver's Army" were caught up short. A sickening realization dawned on a few—"We've been had." Costello had made no effort to point out his activities with Rock Against Racism, although most writers pointed out both that and the antifascist theme of the new album, and reminded fans that his first single, "Less Than Zero," had arisen from Costello's own disgust at the dinnertime TV appearance of white supremacist Oswald Mosley. Some compared the incident to John Lennon's ill-fated comments on a popularity contest between the Beatles and Jesus Christ. Costello had not only confused the enemy—he had also bewildered his most avid admirers.

In England the rock press saw things differently: *Melody Maker* ran just two short pieces without precisely quoting Elvis's remarks, referring only to "allegedly racist and disparaging comments." Writer Roy Trakin, who also attended the press conference, said, "...The liberal branch of the local rock establishment vented its outrage while the rest of us giggled nervously." Complaining of the "carping criticism" Elvis had received, Trakin pointed out the method to Costello's apparent madness ("to goad rather than offend") and appealed to Elvis not to succumb to the "star trappings" already beginning to envelop him. Obviously, the press there was concerned that Elvis was selling out to the American hypocrisy he had so well taunted up to that point; *NME's* headline was "Costello Says Sorry to Hand That Feeds Him" and attributed the Englishmen's poor showing to sheer numbers. According to their account, the story (which they protested was tattled by that bunch of stool pigeons, the Stills entourage) appeared "the very next day" in "every muck-raking newspaper on the East Coast." The account also attributed part of the flak at the news conference to "the presence of some black journalists."

Costello's only comment to *NME:* "Well, you know how it is. One day I love America, the next day I hate it."

NME's writers, though, took real offense at what they considered persecution of their "very own horned toad" and were most concerned about the reports of death threats in these violent United States. Don't worry, El, they said. We know what you meant.

Perhaps it was a case of the hero forcing his worshippers to come to terms with his own mortality. It seemed to some observers as if Costello were really asking for it—challenging someone to knock him senseless. The fact that he himself pointed out the source of his injuries to that Cleveland reporter is also telling. Maybe the occurrence was another extension of Costello's guerrilla tactics, another experiment in seeing how much he could get away with. Perhaps Costello, in the wilds of the Midwest, thought the incident would go unreported. Or maybe Costello, in the fashion of his stage presence, took his worst fears and insecurities and acted them out as grotesquely as possible, as a sort of exorcism. Others who've had more exposure to British culture say that a comment like that would raise no controversy in England, where published quotes that would be viewed as poisonously racist here are printed without a qualm.

But in the U.S. the comments *did* raise controversy, and when Costello began his grueling series of gigs in and around New York (beginning with a Friday night appearance at the Capitol Theatre in Passaic, New Jersey; two shows the next night at the Palladium; and three club dates on Sunday, April 1, at the Lone Star, the Bottom Line, and Great Gildersleeves), he was greeted with pickets from Rock Against Racism. Their placards read "KICK 'IM AGAIN, BONN" and "SEND ELVIS BACK TO COMPUTER SCHOOL." *People* claimed there had been more than 150 death threats. But one of the placard carriers was a most astute observer of the situation—as reported by Schruers, the protesters still liked Elvis but he suggested it would be best if he knew his fans were not "loyal," like sheep, but people who "keep an eye on what he says."

The result of the furor was increased but perhaps justified paranoia from Costello's management. Bodyguards now accompanied the rock star, and U.S. tour manager Des Brown was observed now prominently

The Attractions' very own album with free single—Steve Nieve's Theme Music for Outline of a Hairdo.

onstage, manically scanning audiences for cameras and tape recorders. House bouncers and roadies had a field day, and Hell's Angels accompanied Brown on his "Seek and Destroy" ambushes. Green-fatigued crew members dotted the background, as Costello wrung the last bit of angst from "Lip Service."

The Lone Star date was interesting if only for the cultural contrast: four sickly-pale lads among the leather and spurs. "This playing three clubs is somebody's idea of an April fool, and I think I know who the fool is," said Elvis, pointing at himself. He sang his George Jones collaboration, "Stranger in the House." Shrapnel was the opening group.

He and his own private goon squad had arrived at the Bottom Line by limousine, departing from their normal routine of taking the bus everywhere, and darted past observers at the back door, swinging at

92

Right: The Lone Star Café. One stop among many in the marathon weekend. April Fool's Day, 1979.

photographers along the way. A couple of hundred people waited out front; fewer than sixty would get in.

Tickets had been raffled off to 1,200 lucky people. The radio station holding the contest received about a half million calls.

The lucky few would filter back out, clutching their limited-edition singles ("Talking in the Dark" b/w "Wednesday Week"); and Mick Jagger, with his party, would thrill celebrity seekers by strolling out the back door to a waiting car. A few minutes later Elvis dove through the open door of another sedan, which then sped off, gangland style. On to the Great Gildersleeves.

At the Lone Star he had opened with "I Stand Accused." At the Palladium, after opening with "What's So Funny 'Bout Peace, Love and Understanding?" he commented on the appropriateness of the title of "Accidents Will Happen." Contemporary black American music entertained the throng between sets. Those were the only comments Costello

made after the conference; and apparently no one, in the audiences, at least, asked for anything more.

However, readers of the *Village Voice* and *Rolling Stone* wrote in, expressing much the same reaction the reporters at the conference had shown. One said the actions of this "twerpy punk" who'd come to America to "make big bucks and hire goons to kick the shit out of his audience and then cut down Ray Charles" were excellent reasons for stricter immigration laws. Another called attention to "the real evidence that lies patiently in the grooves." A couple of them were appalled at Bonnie Bramlett, one describing her as a drunken woman who'd punched out a visitor to this country, because she didn't like what he had to say.

The most interesting letter appeared some weeks later, a lone entry after the angry babble in *Rolling Stone*.

> First of all, may I thank you for the review of my son's LP ("Elvis Costello in Love and War," RS 287). It is the most perspicacious of all the reviews in any paper (and I have the cartoon of "El" framed on my wall!). "Oliver's Army" is an important track for me, and your reviewer, Janet Maslin, so quickly picked up on the "white nigger" significance. My grandfather was an Ulster Catholic, and as a child, I lived in an area where bigotry was rife. So we are those white niggers.
>
> This brings me to the disturbing reports that I have seen branding Elvis Costello as a racist. Nothing could be farther from the truth. My own background has meant that I am passionately opposed to any form of prejudice based on religion or race. And El's mother and I were both branded as hotheads and Marxists or anarchists.
>
> So you can see that we don't have any chic, white liberal attitudes (and El has publicly despised the latter many times). This is the water that Elvis has been born and bred in, and he swims in it as naturally as a goldfish. His mother comes from the tough multiracial area of Liverpool, and I think she would still beat the tar out of him if his orthodoxy were in doubt.
>
> Ross MacManus
> Twickenham, England

The letter provides more than a clear, down-to-earth perception of what was to many a mystery: Mr. MacManus's easy handling of a messy situation in language that is both direct and spiced with humor shows us one source of Elvis's environment and heredity. (He'd been even more direct to *NME's* Thrills desk: "... Elvis' mother is a Liverpool lady who'd

Left: Boston, 1978.

beat the fucking tar out of him if she thought he was turning into a racist.")

Jake would later call the incident "a drunken barroom idiocy," but it is an event that will undoubtedly follow Elvis for the rest of his career, even considering the short memory of the average teen. Whether prompted by anger, fatigue, immaturity, or unmitigated obnoxiousness, once he stooped to the language of his adversary, he called his entire career up to that point into question.

For the first time the reviews were less than adulatory. The *New York Times's* John Rockwell summed up the problem admirably. Stating that the passion of the angry young artist is a necessary and "welcome scourge," he also points out that that passion is not to be confused with "the product of an embittered individual [not]...merely twisted pique," or, in fact, "careerism." Costello's survival as an artist, he said, will depend on whether people regard his work as an absolute necessity. And as of the performances of April 1, 1979, "that artistic question was still open."

By late summer 1979 notices about Costello were restricted to far less controversial subjects: his production of the Specials' first album and his movie debut in the comedy *Americathon*. (More on this later.)

Costello appeared in another benefit concert in late 1979, this time a four-day affair that sounded almost like fiction in its scope and ambition. The concert, which resulted from talks between Paul McCartney and U.N. Secretary-General Kurt Waldheim, sought to raise money for an emergency relief fund for the people of Kampuchea (formerly Cambodia). UNICEF and the International Red Cross were the agencies coordinating the monies, and promoter Harvey Goldsmith was behind the scenes as well. Opening December 26 was Queen, and from there the event began snowballing: on the twenty-seventh, Ian Dury and the Blockheads with the Clash; the twenty-eighth featured the Pretenders, the Specials, and no less than the Who; the closing day saw Rockpile, Elvis, Paul McCartney and Wings share the stage before Peter Townshend and the members of Led Zeppelin came up for an extended jam session. *The Concert for the People of Kampuchea* album was released in the spring of 1981.

96

Girls Talk

The reason you've never heard of Jo Marshall is a prime example of why Britannia rules the new wave.

She and her band are warriors on the "front lines," clubs like CBGB and the dance circuit, and even on a weeknight can jolt a jaded New York audience out of their preoccupied ennui to gyrate on the dance floor. Their material is a little like Nick Lowe's: good-timey, tight-knit, upbeat, with lyrics that tease and flirt. But they also have a couple of twists of their own—the steel guitar, played by Ed Bierly (a.k.a. "Ambrose Blam"), which gives a muted country twang, and Jo herself, whose understated mien and strident voice are controlled passion incarnate. Onstage, guitarist Curt Neishloess is a picture of defiant confidence, while bassist Jerry Mitnick (alias "Minique Flambeau") is more like a laid-back New Orleans blues club veteran, even with the skinny glitter tie. He and drummer David Rosenberg provide the basis of the integrated backbeat that gives their sound the unmistakable mark of years of experience.

In the United Kingdom a band like Jo Marshall's would have already attracted the attention of the press, who would then, in turn, alert one of the scores of labels. "No pretense, it's just intense" is the way she describes the CBGB atmosphere, and it could apply to her music as well.

Unfortunately, pretense is in these days. The industry carries on in its business-as-usual way, waiting for the latest import, preferably dressed like Adam and the Ants. Jo Marshall and her band remain unsigned.

Their set consists mostly of songs they wrote together—"Girl Type Girl," "Big Brown Eyes," "Talk to Me"—along with just three cover songs: Jo Jo Zepp's "So Young" and two that Jo proudly states were written for her by Elvis Costello, "True Love" and "Mighty Man."

Sitting in a friendly Brooklyn bar, Capulet's on Montague Street, where she works part-time, she reaches for a cigarette. She is a slight figure in denim jacket and jeans, and the first thing that strikes you about her is the enormous brown eyes, an unblinking brown gaze beneath red bangs. She has those wide-angle cheekbones that make Debbie Harry comparisons inevitable. "It takes a long time," she says amiably. "That's why I'm still a waitress."

"Hey, Jo," says one of the bar's regulars. "You've lost more weight, haven't you? "Look at that *face!*"

"Yeah," she says. "Very Jack Palance."

In the days ahead Marshall and her band have a round of dates at Bond's, the Ritz, cable TV's *Uncle Floyd Show*, and the place where they've begun to feel at home, CBGB. It has taken Marshall fourteen years to arrive at this stage. Since she was a runaway at thirteen, through short-lived bands like Size 5 and the Communists, to her present status of working with a tight, supportive band who have all been in the business long enough to appreciate conquering a small corner of New York, Marshall has somehow escaped the bitterness anyone might have cultivated after long years of hard work and little recognition. She has, instead, an almost indefatigable optimism. That's why her short, and ultimately disappointing, exposure to the big time with Elvis, Nick Lowe, and Jake Riviera failed to unsettle her.

She had been married a year when she heard the Sex Pistols, and it was then she decided to get back into singing. That fall a mutual friend gave Jake Riviera one of her tapes, including her songs "Stop Looking at Her" and "Big Brown Eyes," and he was very impressed. He asked her to stop by the A.R.S.E. offices on Fifty-seventh Street.

She knew he handled Elvis, Nick Lowe, and the rest of that musical "family," but nothing prepared her for the shock when Elvis himself answered the door. He, too, had heard the tape and was impressed, and the two soon became fast friends caught up in admiration for each other's abilities.

Jake had great plans. So ambitious, in fact, that even then she says she knew it wasn't going to be so easy. "He kept saying, 'Don't worry! We'll have you recording for Columbia!'" says Marshall. But it wasn't until the following May, in 1979, that she would begin to work with some of her heroes. Jake arranged for her to go to London to record a demo tape.

"It was great. I had a room, a flight, and pocket money. At first I couldn't believe it. I kept saying, 'Is it Laker, Jake?' He said. 'No, no, it's Pan Am. Just ask Cynthia. She'll fix you up.'"

Somewhat encouraged by the tangible evidence of the Pan Am ticket, she set off with a friend from her band. She'd already had a couple of tip-offs to the kind of trouble that was lying in wait: Riviera and the man who was then her manager didn't get along. Riviera complained about the "plethora of female singers." And there was the gratuitous Riviera patronizing ("Anyone touches your bum and they're fired," he'd said. He'd also insisted on calling her husband, Kai, one morning at two-thirty. "Doesn't he want to know where you're going to be?" he'd demanded.) But she was on her way to London to work with the big boys—and to her surprise, they seemed genuinely interested in helping her out.

"Elvis is such a nice guy," she says. "The piss-on-you attitude comes from Jake." In the ten days that followed, she would get to know Elvis, Nick Lowe, Dave Edmunds, most of the Attractions, Rockpile, Carlene Carter, and the others in their natural habitat.

She had seen Elvis a couple of times since meeting him at A.R.S.E. Once was at his famous Lone Star date in New York, and her opinion of that gig is different from the chronicles of rockbiz. "He was so conciliatory, really catering to the audience," she says. He is no racist, she is sure: They would have long talks about their indebtedness to the early soul and R-&-B singers.

Another meeting before she left for London was at the Mudd Club, when some fans approached Elvis and a woman who was accompanying him, saying, "We'd really be honored if you'd let us take your picture." Marshall was somewhat taken aback when the woman sneered, "Yeah, and we'd really be honored if you'd let us *fuck you!*" This mystery woman turned out to be Fay Hart, Steve Nieve's girlfriend.

When Jo and her friend finally arrived in London, they were met at the airport by Nick Lowe and Carlene Carter who is now his wife. Carter, a member of America's first family of country music, daughter of June Carter, stepdaughter of Johnny Cash, and stepsister of Roseanne Cash, enlisted Lowe's help for several of her own albums, among them *Musical*

Shapes. However, there was no sign of the cowboy Costello. "We had to send Elvis home," they told her. "He got too pissed on Retsina."

"I spent most of those ten days drunk," she says. "Their studio at Acton wasn't open yet, so the first four days we just hung out at Nick's and Elvis's, eating and drinking and talking. They were trying to get the Abbey Road studio but that didn't work out."

Elvis came the next day with a tape recorder and two songs he'd written for her—"Mighty Man" and "True Love." "I sat down in the kitchen and taped 'em for you," he told her. He taught her the songs and later played guitar on the demo tape.

Time's passage (and the haze of alcohol) erode the memory, but certain pictures stand out in her mind, leaving her with a crazy quilt of impressions, some bright, some mottled, connected more by serendipity than the calendar. That afternoon working on the songs, hearing the tape of Elvis in his kitchen playing an acoustic guitar is one. Another has him, another friend, and Marshall all sitting in the back of a limousine rubbernecking like any other tourists after sighting Art Garfunkle on the streets, and another reveals a pasty Elvis going home to sweat out an entire bottle of champagne he'd drunk alone. Yet another has Elvis and Marshall listening to Jo Jo Zepp's "So Young." He urged her to do the song, but Carlene also wanted to record it. They played it over and over until Lowe finally tossed the record out the window. To his regret, it was returned to his mailbox by some passing Samaritan the next day.

She'd heard about the infamous "little black book" but found out it is possibly a less threatening appurtenance than reported. "He carried it with him all the time. He'd write down all kinds of things—dialogue, conversations, and use it to write songs." She remembers him listening to her conversation and suddenly exclaiming, "Stop saying that! Stop saying those things!" and later discovering those contributions to the book.

The patchwork also includes some irresistible bits of imagery, like this one: After a long evening of getting "legless" with her and her friend, Elvis passed out on the floor of her hotel room. "He was happily snoozing away," says Marshall. "I took his glasses off and laid them down beside him. He looked just like this [Marshall strikes the familiar pose of head resting on folded hands]. Just like a little kid." The next day, Elvis was on the phone apologizing for his rude behavior.

Marshall's impressions from the inside are far different from the views

Jo Marshall and band outside CBGB. (Left to right: David Rosenberg, Cut Neishloess, Jo, Jerry Mitnick and Ed Bierly).

of the newshounds clamoring from without. There were three general traits she repeatedly attributed to the F-Beat group: "really nice, really funny, and real drinkers." Their lack of pretension also impressed her. "The genius was so offhand, you'd hardly realize it." Nick Lowe told her he'd learned a lot from Elvis, whom he called "maestro." She remembers two places Elvis liked to eat, the Portobello's hotel restaurant, which was open twenty-four hours, where Elvis particularly liked the quiche and salad, and (appropriately) an Italian restaurant, where he favored the canelloni.

She also liked his wife, Mary ("Very, very pretty, dark hair, beautiful skin... very English. A great sense of style.") She remembers them telling her about coming into customs from France with some very expensive clothes and no one there believing he was who he claimed to be. "They wouldn't believe he was really Elvis Costello," says Marshall. Finally, they submitted him to what they believed would be a conclusive test of identity, telling him to "Make with the toes." He passed.

Mary, too, had that same sense of humor. "She *had* to have one," says Marshall. Marshall regrets never having met their son, Matthew. She spent one evening with Elvis and Mary at the Odeon seeing the J. Geils band, and she and his wife became friends, sharing a couple of girl-talky phone calls.

103

Bebe Buell.

Carlene Carter she remembers as "beautiful. You'd never know she was from one of America's great music families. She wasn't at all condescending. And she writes some really good songs. She was good for girl stuff. We both have a tattoo on the same place," she says, patting her hip. "She has a Japanese tea rose and I have a bird. I remember once we all went to see *The Deer Hunter*. The guys were really into it, but we sat there going, 'Eeee-yuu-uuuck!'"

They told her some of the phrases she'd need to get along: "Berkshire hunt" = *cunt*, "mince pies" = *brown eyes*. Lowe once strode into the room where she was, demanding, "What's all this I hear about Jo Marshall?" Then he walked over and scrutinized her face. "Lovely minces!" he said brightly. "That was the same night he bit me on the side of the head and told me to shut up," she sighs.

Other little images: Elvis walking out the door of her room clutching a bottle of Remy Martin, Stiff photographer Keith Morris having a bottle of the same waiting for her photo session, Mary telling her Elvis had said she was "prettier than Debbie Harry," and Carlene saying she could tell he "dug the flattery" and that the mutual admiration was spurring creativity.

Marshall was the first to use the new studios at Acton, and with Elvis on lead, Lowe on a fretless bass, Steve Nieve on keyboards, and Pete Thomas on drums, they cut the two songs Elvis had written for her. (Bruce Thomas was then away spending time at Paul McCartney's farm in Scotland.)

She also got to know Nieve a bit and his girlfriend Fay Hart, who was also fond of calling herself "Farrah Fuck-It Minor." And here, perhaps, the true soul of the mad Farfisa player is revealed: "He was a great curry cooker. I remember one afternoon he fixed us strawberries, cream, and Grand Marnier."

Perhaps Fay-Farrah's actions are memorable because they were more vociferous. Another time she remembers Fay-Farrah leaning out a window of the Palladium and yelling to the poor, drooling fans below: "Bet you wish you were up here, you fuckers!" Marshall later learned that she, too, was very nice—a little abrasive, perhaps, but nice.

She also remembers seeing Bebe Buell one night at the Mudd Club and Bebe asking how Elvis was doing. Buell and Elvis ended their nine-month liaison the same spring Marshall went to London. A fashion model with an affinity for rock stars, Buell had kept company with Todd Rundgren, Rod Stewart, Jimmy Page, and Iggy Pop before meeting Elvis. In an interview with *Oui* magazine, Buell said that in the spring "he started flipping out on me" and added "I think Elvis derives a lot of inspiration from not being happy."

"It must have been strange for her, to be part of someone's life for a while, and then just nothing," says Marshall. "There was supposedly some material she and Elvis were collaborating on, but nothing ever came of it." Nonetheless, she thinks several songs—"Party Girl" and "This Year's Girl" among them—came from their relationship. Basically, she says, "If he hadn't been married, Bebe wouldn't have been such a taboo."

One night when she was still in London, she and Elvis went out to share a smoke and some talk on the rainy streets. The conversation drifted from music to marriage and what it was like being onstage or on the road with someone waiting at home. "I wouldn't care if my husband slept with the Dallas Cowgirls," she told him. "I've got his clothes. I know he'd have to come back. As long as he comes back, it's OK. Besides, he's not like that," she hedged. "I wish you'd talk to my wife," said Elvis.

All the time she was in London Riviera's reports to her about the future were glowing and enthusiastic. But she kept sensing that something was wrong, and it finally came down to a talk with Carlene in the ladies room to discover the crux of the matter. Because he wanted to do more work with Rockpile, Lowe didn't want to produce her work. "And when I told them that—that all the time you're telling me everything's great but then someone has to take me aside in the bathroom—all the men's eyes go down and they start stammering. Finally Jake told me that if there was anything he could do for me, he would. It was an amicable parting, and I was grateful for his attention." They later asked her not to record the two songs Elvis had written for her.

From her years as the "focal point" in several bands, Marshall is all too accustomed to the problems women face in what may be the last stronghold of machismo—rock & roll. "If the guys don't accept the fact that you're going to be the focal point, there are going to be problems. I mean, sometimes I feel like Eva Peron. But the group I have now is very loving and supportive. We go bowling together." She has very definite views of men's and women's roles: "I think we are a superior race. If I can sing in a band, then come here to work and then clean up the house and *you* can't," she says, glaring at some unseen adversary, "I think that's just because I'm a better person."

From her point of view, being American was little problem, and she suffered no criticism because of it. In fact, she seemed to think it was an advantage. "They all told me the public would think I was exotic because I was American. They really admire American music. It's all ours—apart from the music halls and comedy, they have very little. The rest comes from us."

But she is very aware of the source of the problem between her and Jake Riviera. "He had problems dealing with me on a business level. He could do it on a personal level or a slut level but... you know how it goes. I'd have to be twice as good for them just to get past my tits." She remains completely untroubled by what some might see as her rejection by Riviera. "He's just one geezer," she says.

So it was that Marshall returned to New York, still unsigned but also still very determined. It is unfortunate that her story is, in many ways, typical of American bands in a country with a notorious reputation for allowing its native talent to waste away while the same artist may be inspiring a more lucrative "movement" overseas. Her group appears with some regularity in and around New York, and their compact, driving set is not to be missed. One hopes that Marshall and her band will one day be known outside New York's limited, word-of-mouth circuit.

This Year's Model

After the Bonnie Bramlett incident, an eighteen-month hiatus would pass before Elvis set foot in the United States again, preferring to return to England's friendlier environment. But that didn't mean that his American fans had suffered cold-turkey withdrawal from not seeing their hero; in fact, though there was little written about him in America, his familiar gangly frame was perhaps more widely viewed than ever before through the miracle of the electronic media.

When *Get Happy!!*, with its day-glo, "pre-worn" cover appeared, Elvis himself took to the screen to hawk his wares. With the Attractions bouncing merrily in the background, Elvis firmly warned videoland to *get happy*. "20 songs!! 20!!" reads its ads, and the TV spot reminded one of nothing so much as the used-car ads that sandwiched Elvis. The album also bore a note from producer Nick Lowe, who attested to the disc's aural quality to any consumer who might have thought that the tunes, including the immortal "I Can't Stand Up for Falling Down," were somehow jammed on wax at the sacrifice of the finer points of high fidelity.

The album received mixed reviews, perhaps because critics were taken aback at the sharp contrast of the heavy romantic-dictator theme of *Armed Forces* and the sudden emergence of this happy-tune disc.

Although not as commercially "successful" as *Armed Forces, Get Happy!!* remains the favorite album for many Costello aficionados.

And the summer of 1979 had seen Elvis's movie debut in *Americathon,* one of the then-current rash of cinematic ventures featuring new groups, either in sound tracks or in the flesh. *Rock & Roll High School,* starring the Ramones with music by Nick Lowe, would be released later that summer.

Americathon, like the others, was true to rock & roll ideals of near-anarchic chaos, a true dedication to the lesser points of "culture." The year is 1998 and the United States, on the verge of bankruptcy because of oil cartel demands, has taken to the streets on skateboards and bikes—their cars having become apartments. Written by Firesign Theater's Phillip Proctor and Peter Bergman, the movie starred John Ritter as the newly elected lecherous president, Chet Roosevelt (elected on his "We have nothing on our mind" platform—a takeoff on the old Firesign presidential slogan, "Not Insane"), Harvey Korman as a pill-gobbling Monty Rushmore, and Meat Loaf as a fearless basher of the last gas-guzzler who appears in the telethon the President decides is necessary to raise the cash needed to ward off foreclosure at the hands of an Indian shoe tycoon. Among the other talents on the telethon is a Vietnamese punk rock group. Elvis appears only briefly, as British sensation Earl Manchester performing in front of Buckingham Palace—England has become the fifty-seventh state—but the sound track did give American fans their first chance to buy "Chelsea," and a most appropriate number, "Crawling to the U.S.A." *Rolling Stone* writer Ben Fong-Torres appears briefly as one of the hordes of "Ugly Chinese" descending on the shores of (where else?) southern California.

Another sound track released in May of that year is a stand-out collection of some of the best new bands around. *That Summer* featured Elvis, Richard Hell and the Voidoids, Mink DeVille, the Ramones, Nick Lowe, Patti Smith Group, Eddie and the Hot Rods, Ian Dury, Wreckless Eric and the Boomtown Rats, among others.

In an interview in Dallas in 1978 with Robert Hilburn, which appeared in *Wet* magazine in May of 1981, Elvis said that because of the "very bad experiences" he'd had in England and especially in the United States with the press (including the *Time* interview, which Elvis particularly singled out), he preferred to avoid the print medium altogether and rely on those means in which he could directly face the audience. Perhaps this was the reason for his sudden appearances on the tube and screen.

Promo poster for Get Happy!! ("A great record to dance to but you wouldn't want to live there.")

Promotional videotapes were coming into their own, finding outlets first in rock clubs like Hurrah, Danceteria, and the Ritz in New York City. These clubs like the old Danceteria, sometimes sought to give the crowd a feeling of being "at home," with clusters of couches and pillows around the perhaps twenty closed-circuit monitors dotting the bar's interior. When the live shows commenced downstairs, patrons sometimes elected to languish on the couches and watch the group on monitors as followed by two club employees with Porta-Cams. At breaks in performances, the sets maintained a steady output of eclectic programing, ranging from Japanese commercials, segments of "Leave It to Beaver," old videos of groups live at the club, or one of the new promotional videotapes.

The video may be the Next Big Thing in the entertainment industry, because of the onset of megabucks in the vast cable business and the appearance of the ever more affordable home video recorder, such as the Betamax. The cable question has already been the source of the recent actors' strike, and the current writers' strike also hinges on cable options. Blondie's *Eat to the Beat* was the first album also released on video. At sixty dollars the tape is hardly within the average teen's buying power, but current speculation has it that prices may eventually go as low as fifteen dollars, making the video a tough competitor for the vinyl disc.

Elvis's videos, which find their way onto American screens mostly on such late-night shows as the often-imitated-but-never-truly-captured *Don Kirshner's Rock Concert*, are true delights for the eye-sore. Elvis and the Attractions lip-sync to the tracks over a variety of backgrounds (Elvis eating a plate of chips beside a dock, relaxing beside a shallow pool of water and singing with such ardor that he bounces off his recliner into it—much to his own surprise—coming perilously close to fulfilling the promise of "I Can't Stand Up for Falling Down") while the Attractions frug and pony in the background. A definite departure from the *Saturday Night Live* abrasive appearance, the videos show an Elvis with the superb comic timing of a Chaplin.

Taking Liberties appeared in 1980. A collection of B-sides of 45s and cuts from English LPs not offered before in the United States, the album was met with a haughty attitude by, for one, Robert Palmer of the *New York Times,* who suggested that Mr. Costello had already taken too many liberties.

The Attractions also released a solo album of the same name, with their

"Mad About the Wrong Boy" countering Nieve's "Sad About Girls."

The EP/45 market was not ignored, either, with the appearances of, first, several cuts from *Armed Forces* on Radar, and then the EPs on F-Beat. *High Fidelity* (both 7- and 12- inch), with "Getting Mighty Crowded" by Van McCoy and "Clowntime is Over" (a new slower version on 12-inch) and *New Amsterdam* with "Dr. Luther's Assistant," "Ghost Town," and "Just a Memory" are among them.

Also in 1979 Elvis appeared on one of his heroes' albums, George Jones's *My Very Special Guests*, singing "Stranger in the House," which was also released as a single, b/w Jones's "A Drunk Can't Be a Man." The video special of the same name appeared on cable television much later, featuring a puffy Elvis, who was recuperating from the mumps. (Current speculation is that Costello's next album will be all country.)

Somehow he and the Attractions also found the time for another extensive tour of England, drawing the same enthusiastic crowds; but by now the rock press's ardor had cooled a bit. Like London's *Sunday Times* critic Derek Jewell, who hoped that Costello would "break out of category." Jewell, however, seems more concerned with the welfare of an artist he admires in danger of becoming trapped by his image of one "dancing on the grave of Hollywood's fallen dreams hallowed by suburbia's Laureate." "He should relax a bit, and I hope he gets happier," he says in another passage. "Life is tough but not all of it. If his range widens, and some songs are more sensitively arranged, he could become a major artist of the Eighties."

As if in response, Elvis's latest album to date, *Trust*, was released in January of 1981. The album's cover and sleeve brought out the best of Elvis's film noir–Bogey aspects. On the cover he peers over his new dark glasses, eyebrows arched in incredulity, like someone who knows more than he's telling. Cigarette smoke curls in the background. The sleeve's photos are fit for pinups: Elvis in fedora and dark glasses hugging his overcoat (and mystique) close. The back features a grainy pic of Elvis in front of a full orchestra, "EC" emblazoned on their music stands. (Is that Nick Lowe on sax?) Shades of Joe Loss.

He'd done it again—broken out onto untrodden ground, waking up fans and critics and the unconverted. *Trust* is the most important album since *Armed Forces*, another recording so dense in subject matter, tricky concourses, twisted cliches, and offhand brilliance that if it weren't for the addictive hooks, a first-time listening might prove intimidating. Squeeze's

A poster revealing the source of the photograph on the cover of Get Happy!!

Glenn Tilbrook is allowed a spot as guest artist, and his smooth, bright voice is an appropriate foil for Costello's rough and ragged singing on "From a Whisper to a Scream." Far from backing off from the controversial "emotional fascism" thrust, "White Knuckles on Black and Blue Skin" is a graphic example of the idea pared down to its minimal image. "Didn't mean to hit her/But she just kept laughing," says Costello, almost matter-of-factly. Again the ambiguous "you and me"—mixed so that identities are masked, and even the victim/victor line is a gray one.

"New Lace Sleeves," though, is most characteristic of the new direction

114

Costello explores on *Trust*. Bruce Thomas's bass taking a leading instrumental role beneath the lyrical ballad, Elvis's voice climbs over and around the spare, precise Attractions. "Clubland" is a glimpse backstage of the small and midsize club circuit that has so colored the lives of both Elvis and his father, with oblique references to the sleepless performers against a backdrop of the underworld ("Have you ever been had/In Clubland?")

Perhaps the most impressive showing is Steve Nieve, whose "spookiness" has matured from grade-B thriller theme to the more sophisticated hesitation and complexity of a Hitchcock. Pete Thomas, too, provides great range in the all-important backbeat, terse and muted, aggressive and retiring. They've progressed from a singer with a backup to an integrated group whose individual contributions are as distinctive as the whole.

Almost before anyone had a chance to hear the album they were on tour again, from the West Coast to New York. By this time, though, journalists made a few futile attempts at interviews, most simply kept at a respectful distance and relied on record reviews.

Thus it was something of a shock when Costello, soon after his New York appearance, cropped up on the Tom Snyder show. According to a Columbia spokesperson, the interview had come about as a result of an inexperienced person on Snyder's staff who'd pestered them for almost two years "in a very naive way." When Columbia and Alan Frey, Costello's U.S. tour manager, approached the Costello camp, he accepted, much to their surprise. But the Columbia source also said there was an element of "black humor" involved—Elvis could go on and not worry about the kinds of serious questions and the expectations of serious responses that most reporters would require of him. Tom Snyder would certainly be anything but that.

Snyder, still smarting from an "unpleasant" interview with John Lydon, reportedly approached the conversation with some trepidation. But he ended up thanking Elvis for the "enjoyable" talk.

Whether or not Snyder even knew of the Bramlett incident is unclear, but he asked nothing about it in the seven-minute talk. Instead, Costello was at his funniest, describing the early days of going into executives' offices ready to confront them with his battery of songs while they chatted on the phone ("He's going, 'Yes, Darling, I'll be home around eight, no, lamb casserole will be great' ..."). In an almost Dan Akroyd–ish manner, Snyder blithely swung from vague and general to very personal, asking both if he'd learned to control his anger and if he loved his father. Costello said yes to the latter, but when Snyder asked him if he thought he'd matured, Costello demurred, saying it sounded "like cheese or something." After requesting Snyder to "do the funny eyebrows," he took to the stage to sing "You'd Better Watch Your Step."

Costello was relaxing at a Providence, Rhode Island, hotel bar and chatting with fans some days after the Snyder interview when *Aquarian* reporter "Everynight" Charley Crespo happened on the scene, having been brought there by a friend. In the men's room, he encounterd Jake Riviera and struck up a conversation with him, which Crespo says ranged to the absurd.

Riviera was venting his displeasure with American culture, from its hamburgers to its newspapers (although he took care to point out that he didn't hate *all* Americans—he'd married one) to its talk-show hosts, Tom Snyder in particular. Crespo said Riviera sometimes made incomprehensible remarks, like the following: Complaining that Snyder "knows about as much about music as I do about bringing the hostages home on a Barbra Streisand scale," Riviera also was convinced that in the aftermath of the interview, half the American population probably thought Costello was arrogant and the other half thought he was mellow. Crespo countered that probably half the population had never heard of Elvis. It was then that Jake demanded to know Crespo's occupation. When he wouldn't answer, Riviera became angry and, according to Crespo, hoisted him by his lapels and called him a wimp and a disgrace to his country for not answering.

Crespo said Riviera then told his friend what he thought was the "ultimate insult": "Your friend is so *American,*" said Riviera. Crespo also said he thinks that Riviera's idea of the typical American—aggressive, pushy—would also aptly describe Riviera.

Costello sat a few feet away during the incident and chatted with fans.

"Costello has indeed mellowed," Crespo wrote. "Riviera, on the other hand, apparently hasn't."

In London in the spring, turmoil once again erupted, this time racial conflicts in the Brixton area. Ironically, it is also the site of Costello's 1978 Rock Against Racism concert and the home base of the blue-beat Two-Tone label, whose emphasis is on the peaceful cohabitation of all races and has produced such groups as the Specials and Selecter. As groups of blacks and whites took to the streets, largely in protest of police

116

practices, they warned that the trouble at Brixton was a sign of things to come unless Britain accepted the ancestors of the conquered lands of the Empire as the native-born English citizens they were, entitled to equal jobs and housing.

The face of the new has also changed, and now groups like Adam and the Ants, Spandau Ballet, Visage, and Ultra Vox, characterized by elaborate costumes and an almost commedia dell' arte delivery, occupy the press. Punk rock in the United States has sunk to the almost universally critically deplored Dead Kennedys from the West Coast, where a new, more serious flirtation with goon rock and neo-Nazism seems to be developing. Slam dancing is replacing the pogo.

Once again New York seems only too willing to ignore its own, and groups like Jo Marshall's still struggle. Stiff now harnesses the energy of the Plasmatics, Lene Lovich, and Madness for home consumption. The U.K. keeps its emphasis on new wave as mainstream: The United States seems to be taking a breather from an onslaught it has not yet fully absorbed.

Meanwhile, Costello's songs play on AM but probably not enough to please him, and he's still a force that no one's quite been able to touch. They long ago eclipsed the Bay City Rollers, but, thank God, they're still not satisfied. Only four years ago Elvis burst on the scene with the aggressive impatience of a dying man. It's as if he's just now realizing he has more time than that.

Promo poster for Get Happy.

Discography

ELVIS DISCS

LPs are listed in capitals.

ps-picture sleeve

Less Than Zero/Radio Sweetheart (ps)	Stiff	BUY-11	(UK)	3/77

"Less Than Zero" is different from album cut

Alison/Welcome to the Working Week (ps)	Stiff	BUY-14	(UK)	5/77
Red Shoes/Mystery Dance	Stiff	BUY-15	(UK)	7/77
MY AIM IS TRUE	Stiff	SEEZ-3LP	(UK)	7/77
	Columbia	35037	(US)	

First edition of U.K. version distributed by Island in b-&-w photo on front, choice of four colors on back: later are green, orange, and black posterization. Initially sold with pamphlet inviting buyer to have a copy sent free to a friend. U.S. has red, yellow, and black front; first edition of back is yellow, later white. U.S. also adds "Watching the Detectives."

1) Welcome to the Working Week, Miracle Man, No Dancing, Blame It On Cain, Alison, Sneaky Feelings; 2) Red Shoes, Less Than Zero, Mystery Dance, Pay It Back, I'm Not Angry, Waiting for the End of the World.

Alison/Miracle Man	Columbia	3-10641	(US)

String synthesizer added to "Alison"; "Miracle Man" is live from London and has appeared nowhere else.

Watching the Detectives	Stiff (ps)	BUY-20	(UK)
Blame It on Cain/Mystery Dance	Columbia	3-10696	(US)

Elvis backed by members of the Rumour on "Detectives"; "Cain" and "Mystery Dance" are live in London and appear nowhere else.

Alison/Watching the Detectives	Columbia	3-10705	(US)

Same version of "Alison" as previous Columbia single.

LIVE AT THE EL MOCAMBO	Columbia	CDN-10C	(Can)

Promo live LP: edition of 500. Counterfeit LP almost identical.

1) Mystery Dance, Waiting for the End of the World, Welcome to the Working Week, Less Than Zero (Dallas version), The Beat, Lip Service, Chelsea, Little Triggers, Radio Radio; 2) Lipstick Vogue, Watching the Detectives, Miracle Man, You Belong to Me, Pump It Up.

(I Don't Want to Go to) Chelsea/ You Belong to Me (ps)	Radar	ADA-3	(UK)	3/78

My sincere thanks to Emanuel Maris, whose enormous effort enabled me to compile this discography.

THIS YEAR'S MODEL	Radar	RAD-3	(UK)	3/78
	Columbia	35331	(US)	

"Misprint" cover in U.K., with first 5,000 including single "Stranger in the House" b/w cover version of "Neat, Neat, Neat" (SAM 83). U.S. version has on-center cover with different picture; "Night Rally" and "Chelsea" are replaced with "Radio Radio," and first edition has "Costello" instead of Columbia on label. Recent F-Beat U.K. reissue (XXLP-4) prints cover correctly.

1) No Action, This Year's Girl, The Beat, Pump It Up, Little Triggers, You Belong to Me; 2) Hand in Hand, Chelsea, Lip Service, Living in Paradise, Lipstick Vogue, Night Rally.

Pump It Up/Big Tears (ps)	Radar	ADA-10	(UK)	6/78

"Big Tears" features Mick Jones on guitar.

Costello/Lowe/DeVille	Columbia	AS443		

Promo only, 12" clear orange vinyl. Released with 1978 tour. Collaboration with Capitol, DeVille's label. Counterfeit detectable by lack of spine info.

1) Radio (Elvis), Cruel to be Kind (Lowe) (Columbia label); 2) Soul Twist (DeVille) (Capitol label).

This Year's Girl/Big Tears	Columbia	10762	(US)	
Radio Radio/Tiny Steps (ps)	Radar	ADA-24	(UK)	10/78

12" promo version also printed, though not originally distributed, with plain Radar sleeve.

American Squirm/Peace, Love and Understanding (ps)	Radar	ADA-26	(UK)	10/78

A side by Nick Lowe; B side by Nick Lowe and His Sounds (Elvis and the Attractions).

Talking in the Dark/Wednesday Week (ps)	Radar	RG-1	(UK)	12/78

Free single given at London's Dominion Christmas concert, 1978, and at all three 3/1/79 shows in New York.

Oliver's Army/My Funny Valentine (ps)	Radar	ADA-31	(UK)	1/79
My Funny Valentine/Peace, Love and Understanding	Columbia	AE7-1172	(US)	

Promo only: red vinyl with floating hearts label. Counterfeit has removed "Columbia" from label and has picture sleeve.

ARMED FORCES	Radar	RAD-15	(UK)	2/79
	Columbia	JC-35709	(US)	

U.K. has gatefold cover, postcards, and free "Live at Hollywood High" single (SAM 90) with "Alison," "Watching the Detectives," and "Accidents Will Happen." There is also a U.S. promo 12" single (Col. AS529) in plain sleeve. Later editions had regular pocket covers. U.S. has drip graphic cover, includes single (Col. AE71171) with same picture sleeve; "Peace, Love and Understanding" (added at end of side 2) replaces "Sunday's Best."

1) Accidents Will Happen, Senior Service, Oliver's Army, Big Boys, Green Shirt, Party

Girl; 2) Goon Squad, Busy Bodies, Sunday's Best, Moods for Moderns, Chemistry Class, Two Little Hitlers.

Accidents Will Happen/ Sunday's Best	Columbia	3-10919	(US)	
Accidents Will Happen/Talking in the Dark/Wednesday Week	Radar	ADA-35	(UK)	3/79

Two picture sleeves—first has different picture from second, and is inside out.

I Can't Stand Up (For Falling Down)/	2-Tone	CHS-TT7	(UK)
Girls Talk	F-Beat (with ps)	XX1	(UK)
	Columbia	1-11194	(US)

13,000 copies pressed on 2-Tone after Riviera abandoned Radar with Costello and Lowe but not distributed, probably because this small label could not afford impending suit by WEA (which bought Radar). Riviera formed F-Beat, and later free copies were given to the audience at London's Rainbow Theatre; remaining were sold at N.Y. Palladium 1981 concerts for $3.00 each.

GET HAPPY!!	F-Beat	XXLP-1	(UK)	3/80
	Columbia	JC36347	(US)	

U.K. has "pre-worn" cover, as if pulled out of stack many times; some have b-&-w poster with different slogans (e.g. "Get Lost," etc.); U.S. is plain, without poster. Twenty songs. Cover listing reverses order of sides.

1) Love for Tender, Opportunity, The Impostor, Secondary Modern, King Horse, Possession, Man Called Uncle, Clowntime Is Over, New Amsterdam, High Fidelity, 2) I Can't Stand Up (For Falling Down), Black and White World, 5ive Gears in Reverse, B-Movie, Motel Matches, Human Touch, Beaten to the Punch, Temptation, I Stand Accused, Riot Act.

GET HAPPY!!	F-Beat	XXPROMO 1(UK)

Double promo with b-&-w cover and F-Beat logo. Two discs at 45 rpm, all 20 songs, five to a side. Includes 8-x-10 still and same poster as above.

High Fidelity/Getting Mighty Crowded (ps)	F-Beat	XX3	(UK)
High Fidelity/Getting Mighty Crowded/Clowntime Is Over (ps)	F-Beat	XX3T	

12" EP, with a different, slower "Clowntime."

New Amsterdam/Dr. Luther's Assistant (ps)	F-Beat	XX5	(UK)	6/80
New Amsterdam/ Dr. Luther's Assistant/Ghost Train/Just a Memory (ps)	F-Beat	XX5E	(UK)	6/80

Same songs on picture disc (F-Beat XX5P). Different picture from picture sleeve of XX5E.

I Can't Stand Up.../ Girls Talk/Secondary Modern/ King Horse (ps)	Columbia	1-11251	(US)

7" EP.

TAKING LIBERTIES	Columbia	JC36839	(US)	10/80

Compilation of rarities and B sides.

1) Clean Money, Girls Talk, Talking in the Dark, Radio Sweetheart, Black and White World #2, Big Tears, Just a Memory, Night Rally, Stranger in the House, Clowntime #2; 2) Getting Mighty Crowded, Hoover Factory, Tiny Steps, Chelsea, Dr. Luther's Assistant, Sunday's Best, Crawling to the USA, Wednesday Week, My Funny Valentine, Ghost Train.

10 BLOODY MARYS AND 10 HOW'S YOUR FATHERS	Columbia	XXC-6	(UK)	10/80

Issued in U.K. as cassette only, similar to *Taking Liberties*. "Peace, Love and Understanding," "Watching the Detectives," and "Radio Radio" replace "Sunday's Best," "Chelsea," and "Night Rally." Leaves only "Black and White World #2" unavailable in the U.K. on disc.

Taking Liberties	Columbia	AS847	(US)

12" promo only.

1) Clean Money, Radio Sweetheart; 2) Getting Mighty Crowded, Talking in the Dark.

New Amsterdam/Wednesday Week	Columbia	1-11284	(US)
Getting Mighty Crowded/Radio Sweetheart	Columbia	1-11389	(US)
Clubland/ Clean Money/Hoover Factory (ps)	F-Beat	XX12	(UK)

TRUST	F-Beat	XXLP 11	(UK)	1/81
	Columbia	JC37051	(US)	

U.K. and U.S. exactly the same(!) Japanese import offers lyrics.

1) Clubland, Lovers Walk, You'll Never Be a Man, Pretty Words, Strict Time, Luxembourg, Watch Your Step; 2) New Lace Sleeves, From a Whisper to a Scream, Different Finger, White Knuckles, Shot with His Own Gun, Fish and Chip Paper, Big Sister's Clothes.

Watch Your Step/Luxembourg (ps)	Columbia	11-60519	(US)
From a Whisper to a Scream/ Luxembourg (ps)	F-Beat	XX14	(UK)
Watch Your Step/Tom Snyder Interview (2/4/81)	Columbia	AS958	(US)

12" promo only.

RELATED ALBUMS

AMERICATHON	CBS	70172	(UK)	79
		JC36174	(US)	

Film soundtrack with "Chelsea" and first appearance of "Crawling to the USA."

A BUNCH OF STIFFS	Stiff	SEEZ-2	(UK)	77

Sampler with "Less Than Zero." Contains unlisted, rare Graham Parker cut.

CONCERT FOR THE PEOPLE OF KAMPUCHEA	Atlantic	2-7005	(US)	3/81

"The Impostor" (live) from 12/26/79 concert.

HITS GREATEST STIFFS	Stiff	FIST-1	(UK)	10/77

Sampler contains "Radio Sweetheart." Interesting note: One side of inner sleeve has a grid of LP cover repros of artists on *other* labels whom Stiff recommends (Abba, Petty, Chiswick Sampler, Presley Sun Collection, Beefheart, and others).

Excerpts from Stiff singles	Stiff	FREEBIE-2	(UK)	78

7", 33-rpm promo includes extracts from three Costello tracks: "Alison," "Red Shoes," and "Watching the Detectives."

LIVE STIFFS LIVE	Stiff	GET-1	(UK)	78
	Arista	STF50445	(US)	
	EMI	MFP50445	(UK)	

Three Elvis cuts: "Miracle Man," David & Bacharach's "I Just Don't Know What to do with Myself," and with chorus on Dury anthem, "Sex & Drugs & Rock & Roll." EMI reissue has different cover from Arista and Stiff.

MY VERY SPECIAL GUESTS	Epic	35544	(US)	79

George Jones LP with Jones & Costello duet, "Stranger in the House."

Stranger in the House/A Drunk Can't Be a Man (George Jones)	Epic	3EPC8560	(UK)

ROCK AGAINST RACISM'S GREATEST HITS	Virgin	RAR1-LP	(UK)	2/81

"Goon Squad." Also includes alternate version of the Clash's "Hammersmith Palais."

THAT SUMMER	Arista/Spart	1088		5/79

Music featured in film of same name. Elvis's "Chelsea" and "Watching the Detectives."

The Attractions

MAD ABOUT THE WRONG BOY	F-Beat	XXLP8	(UK)

1) Arms Race, Damage, Little Misunderstanding, Straight Jacket, Mad About the Wrong Boy, Motorworld, On the Third Stroke, Slow Patience; 2) La-la-la-la-la Loved You, Single Girl, Lonesome Little Town, Taste of Poison, Arms Race, High-Rise Housewife, Talk About Me, Sad About Girls, Camera Camera. Comes with Steve Nieve's *Theme Music for Outline of a Hairdo* (COMB-1) (7" with ps): 1) Outline of a Hairdo, Page One of a Dead Girl's Diary; 2) Sparrow Crap, The Tapdancer.

Single Girl/Slow Patience (ps)	F-Beat	XX7	(UK)
Arms Race/Lonesome Little Towns (ps)	F-Beat	XX10	(UK)

The Specials

THE SPECIALS	2-Tone	5001	(UK)	79
	Chrysalis	1265	(US)	

Elvis produced.

Message to You Rudy/Niteklub	2-Tone	5	(UK)

Elvis produced.

Squeeze

EAST SIDE STORY	A&M	4854	(US)	81

Elvis produced. Also provided backing vocals on "Tempted" and "There's No Tomorrow."

Tempted/Trust	A&M	2345	(US)

Elvis produced; B side not on album.

Tempted/Yap Yap Yap	A&M	8147

Elvis produced A side.

BOOTLEGS

(song titles are abbreviated)

ACCIDENTS	Impossible	2-28

1978 show with Nick Lowe on bass. Reissued as *Elvis Costello*, with color cover (Toasted 2s903).

1) Stranger, Oliver, Accidents, Waiting, No Action; 2) TYGirl, Lip Service, Zero, Big Tears, Hand in Hand; 3) The Beat, Red Shoes, Alison, Miracle Man, Chelsea; 4) Mystery Dance, Detectives, You Belong to Me, Pump It Up.

ARMED AND DANGEROUS	Impossible	1-32

1) Welcome, Red Shoes, Waiting, No Action, The Beat, Zero, Radio, You Belong to Me; 2) Lipstick, Detectives, Pump It Up, Mystery Dance, No Dancing. Reissued as one of two discs in *Exit*, with color cover (Toasted. 2s919).

BIG OPPORTUNITY		79-116/117

1) Opportunity, Moods, Green Shirt, Party Girl, Girls School, Accidents; Big Boys, Goon Squad, Oliver, Peace, Radio.

Cornered
(Gatefold ps)

1) Wave a White Flag, Cheap Reward; 2) Hoover Factory, Really Mystified.

Side-1 songs are acoustic solo demos for Radio London, spring 1977. "Hoover Factory" is electric solo demo for Capitol Radio, fall 1977; "Really Mystified" is from BBC, fall 1978.

DELUXE		GHL 25

1) Love for Tender, Human Touch, The Impostor, Secondary Modern, Girls Talk, King Horse, Temptation, Opportunity, 5ive Gears; 2) Can't Stand Up, Clowntime, Possession, B-Movie, Accused, Motel Matches, Hi Fidelity.

Elvis Costello (ps)	Cowboy Discs	Nick 1

EP contains: 1) Stranger (demo); 2) I Just Don't Know (demo), Honky Tonk Blues (live).

ELVIS GOES TO WASHINGTON	Pacifist	7978

DAVE EDMUNDS AND FRIENDS
DON'T

1) Pump It Up/Waiting/No Action medley, Zero, The Beat; 2) Chelsea, Hand in Hand, Radio, You Belong to Me, Lipstick; 3) Mystery Dance, Miracle Man, Chemistry. Reissued as *Elvis Visits Washington* (Phoenix 44779), with color cover. Side 4 is Rockpile broadcast from the Bottom Line with Keith Richards.

50,000,000 ELVIS FANS CAN'T BE WRONG   EL-5000 (1498)

1) Hoover Factory, You Belong, Radio, Mystery Dance, Red Shoes, Zero, Cain, Alison, Chelsea, Detectives, Lip Service; 2) Detectives, Tiny Steps, Big Tears, Roadette's Song, Paradise, Triggers. All but last three are demos, solo and accompanied. Last three are live at Four Ackers Club, Marcy, N.Y., 1977; 3) Welcome, Red Shoes, Hand in Hand, Waiting, No Action, Zero, No Dancing, Big Tears, Triggers, Radio; 4) You Belong, Pump It Up, Lipstick, Detectives, Miracle Man, Mystery Dance. Live at the Agora, Cleveland, 12/5/77. Cover parody of Presley album of same name.

HATE YOU LIVE

1) Goon Squaq, Big Opportunity, Oliver's Army, Busy Bodies, Two Little Hitlers, Green Shirt, Big Boys, Party Girl; 2) Wednesday Week, Talking in the Dark, Stranger in the House, Neat Neat Neat, Radio Sweetheart, Night Rally, My Funny Valentine. Bootleg comp. of studio cuts on 45s.

HIS FIRST KORNYPHONE RECORD   TAKRL 928

1) Welcome, Red Shoes, Waiting, No Action, Zero, The Beat; 2) Roadette Song, Cain, Triggers, Radio (fades out). (From the Hot Club, Philadelphia?).

Honky Tonk Demos (ps)   Compact   Actla   93610

7" EP contains: 1) Lip Service, Jump Up, Mystery Dance; 2) Wave a White Flag, Cain, Poison Moon. Costello accompanies himself on guitar for these demos. Early version of "Lip Service" to the tune of "Stranger in the House." Extra stanza on "Mystery Dance": "I'm gonna walk right up to Heaven, dodging the lightning rods/I'm gonna have this very personal conversation with God/I said 'You got the information, why don't you say so?'/He said, 'Well, I been around but I still don't know.'" Other songs are unreleased so far.

KORNYPHONE RADIO HOUR   TAKRL 9-01

1) Mystery Dance, Waiting, Welcome, Zero, Lip Service; 2) Triggers, Radio, Lipstick, Detectives, Heart of the City, Miracle Man. Culled from El Mocambo broadcast. Re-released as *Saturated* (Excitable L1518-1); also as one of two discs in *Exit* with color cover (Toasted, 2s919).

THE LAST FOXTROT   Rubber Robot   002

1) Goon Squad, Zero, Chelsea, Pump It Up, Radio, Lipstick, Detectives; 2) Party Girl, Not Angry (rest of side 2 is Rockpile songs from opening set).

Last Year's Model (ps)   Time Warp   1

7" EP: 1) Mystery Dance, Waiting; 2) Welcome, Radio. Culled from El Mocambo broadcast.

LIVE AT THE PALOMINO   Centrifugal   12CENT03

1) Big Boys, Hand in Hand, Opportunity, Accidents, Goon Squad; 2) Hitlers, The Beat, Green Shirt, Radio; 3) Stranger, Psycho, If I Could Put Them All Together (I'd Have You), Motel Matches; 4) He'll Have to Go, Girls Talk, Alison, Chelsea, Mystery Dance. John McPhee joins band from third side on.

OUR AIM IS TRUE Stiff S-3230

> 1) Third Rate Romance, Paradise, Radio Soul (takes 1 and 2), Pay It Back, Imagination Is a Powerful Deceiver (1 and 2); 2) Imagination #3, Third Rate Romance #2, Knockin' on Heaven's Door, I'm Packing Up (1 and 2), (Please Mister) Don't Stop the Band, I Just Don't Know. May be pirate of record sent in response to pamphlet suggestion in *My Aim Is True;* may be bootleg. Theoretically, Elvis backed by members of Rumour. Clear vinyl. French label.

Radio Blast Bang 4

(color Xerox ps)

> 7" EP contains: 1) B-Movie, Possession; 2) High Fidelity, Beaten to the Punch. All are BBC Radio broadcasts, 1980.

RADIO RADIO EC 2240

> 1) Mystery Dance, Waiting, Wednesday Week, Zero, The Beat, Lip Service; 2) Chelsea, Triggers, Radio, Lipstick, Detectives, Pump It Up. Culled from El Mocambo broadcast.

SOMETHING NEW LIE-003

> 1) Temptation, Help Me, Accused, One More Heartache, Secondary Modern, Hi Fidelity, Lipstick, Waiting; 2) Don't Look Back, Girls Talk, Detectives, You Belong, Oliver, Pump It Up. King Biscuit Flower Hour broadcast, 1980, with Martin Belmont on second guitar as Steve Nieve recuperates from car accident.

A Super EP Super 101

> 1) Chelsea, You Belong; 2) Paradise, Hoover Factory. Culled from *50,000,000 Elvis Fans.*

WE'RE ALL CREEPS #3

> 1) Mystery Dance, Waiting, Night Rally, No Action, Zero; 2) The Beat, Chelsea, TYGirl, Triggers.

On early records there are messages inscribed in the area between the label and the last song. They are listed here following catalog numbers.

(BUY-11)	A side:	"Elvis is King"
	B side:	"Elvis is King on this side too"
(BUY-14)	A side:	"Elvis joins the FBI"
	B side:	"Elvis is King"
(BUY-15)	A side:	"Help us hype the Elvis"
	B side:	"Larger than life and more fun than people—Elvis"
(BUY-20)	A side	"I think you know what I mean"
	B side:	"Little triggers/big tears"
(RADAR ADA 12)	1:	"You've got to hand it to Bruce"
	2:	"His bottle's gone"
(RADAR ADA 24)	2:	"No Message"
(ADA 31)	2:	"Happy 14th"
(ADA 35)	1:	"A Porky Prime cut will happen"

(RAD-3)   "Special pressing 003. Ring 434-3232 and ask Moira for your special prize." (Callers received an autographed, b&w still and a button that read "Elvis Costello: Born in 1954 for 1978. This Year's Model.")

KNOWN COVER VERSIONS PERFORMED AND/OR RECORDED BY ELVIS:

Peace, Love and Understanding (Lowe), I Can't Stand Up (Banks/Jones), (S)He's Got You (H. Cochran), Little Sister (Pomus/Schuman), My Funny Valentine (Rodgers/Hart), He'll Have to Go (Allison/Allison), If I Could Put Them All Together (I'd Have You) (Stevens), Knockin' on Heaven's Door (Dylan), Third Rate Romance (Low Rent Rendezvous) (Smith), Neat Neat Neat (James), Gloomy Sunday (Lewis/Seress), Help Me (Gatlin), I Stand Accused (Colton/Smith), Don't Look Back (Robinson/White), Psycho, The Roadette Song (Dury/Hardy), One More Heartache (Robinson/White), I Just Don't Know What to Do with Myself (Bacharach-David), I Need Your Love So Bad (Erma Thomas).

ELVIS COSTELLO VIDEOS

Oliver's Army; Pump It Up; Peace, Love and Understanding; Chelsea; Love for Tender; High Fidelity.

Appeared as a collection on a single telecast of the U.S. TV show *Rockworld*.

Known Costello songs that he has yet to record: "That's What Friends Are For," "Mighty Man," "True Love."

Elvis' next move: A country LP with George Jones, reportedly titled *Almost Blue*.

127

Acknowledgments

Elvis Costello: A Singing Dictionary, New York: Warner Bros. Publications, Inc., 1980. *The New Music,* by Glenn A. Baker and Stuart Cope. London: Ring Books, 1980. *Volume: International Discography of the New Wave*, B. George et.al., eds. New York: One Ten Records, 1980. *Rock Family Trees*, by Peter Frame. New York: Quick Fox, 1979. *Contemporary Music Almanac 1980/81,* Ronald Zalkind, ed. New York: Schirmer Books, 1981.

Arrington, Carl, *New York Post,* 12/14/77; Baker, Norman, *NME,* 4/7/79; Broomfield, Christopher, *Nineteen* (London), 7/78; Brown, Mick, *Times* (London), 78; Carr, Tim, *Minneapolis Tribune,* 2/16/78; Cohen, Debra Rae, *Soho Weekly News,* 2/4/81; Connelly, Christopher, *Rolling Stone,* 4/2/81; Crespo, Charley, *Aquarian,* 2/18/81; Denselow, Robin, *Guardian* (London), 8/16/77; Fixmer, Bob, *Madison* (Wisc.) *Capitol Times,* 4/21/78; Fong-Torres, Ben, *Rolling Stone,* 9/6/79; Frith, Simon, *Village Voice,* 12/26/77; Geng, Veronica, *The New Yorker,* 7/27/79; Gilmore, Mikal, *Rolling Stone,* 3/25/.79; Grabel, Richard, *NME,* 2/14/81; Hilburn, Robert, *Wet,* 5/81; Jackson, Richard, *Record Collector,* 12/80; Jewell, Derek, *Times* (London), 10/5/80; Johnson, James *Evening Standard* (London), 8/9/77; Jones, Allan, *Melody Maker,* 8/6/77, 10/7/77; Kent, Nick, *NME,* 8/27/77, 3/25/78; King, Wayne, *Trouser Press,* 5/81;Kirkeby, Marc, *Village Voice,* 4/2/79; Leogrande, Ernest, *Daily News,* 12/15/77, 3/3/79, 2/6/81; Levin, Angela, *The Observer,* 16/2/81; Lipper, Hal, *Dayton Daily News,* 3/15/79; MacDonald, Patrick, *Seattle Times,* 2/7/79; Marcus, Greil, *Rolling Stone,* 1/12/78; Maslin, Janet, *Rolling Stone,* 3/22/79; Miller, Jim, *New Times,* 5/29/78; Milward, John, *Chicago Sun-Times,* 4/24/78; Morse, Steve, *Boston Globe,* 5/6/78; Murray, Charles Shaer, *NME,* 1/8/78; Oppel, Pete, *Dallas Morning News,* 6/4/78; Palmer, Robert, *New York Times,* 9/19/80, 1/28/81, 2/2/81, 4/15/81; Patoski, Joe Nick, *Austin American Statesman,* 5/25/78; Penman, Ian, *NME,* 1/24/81; Rachliss, Kit, *Rolling Stone,* 6/29/78, *Village Voice,* 1/22/79; Rein, Richard K., *People,* 4/23/79; Rockwell, John, *New York Times,* 12/15/77, 5/5/78, 1/3/79; Rose, Frank, *Village Voice,* 4/9/79; Ross, Bob, *St. Petersburg (Fla.) Times,* 5/16/78; Rudis, Al, *Chicago Sun Times,* 12/5/77; Sasfy, Joseph, *Washington Post,* 12/25/77; Schruers, Fred, *Rolling Stone,* 5/17/79; Schwartz, Tony, *Newsweek,* 5/8/78; Scott, Jane, *Cleveland Plain Dealer,* 3/22/79; Trakin, Roy, *Melody Maker,* 4/14/79; Tucker, Ken, *Rolling Stone,* 4/2/81; *L.A. Herald Examiner,* 2/19/79; Zito, Tom, *Washington Post,* 12/9/77; Zuckerman, Ed, *Rolling Stone,* 12/14/78; "Elvis Costello: Gut Emotions," (*Time,* 12/26/77); *Oui* interview with Bebe Buell (5/80); *L.A. Times* report on the Grammys (2/20/79); "The Other Elvis" *Daily Mirror* (London) 8/13/77; Stiff rejection letter (*Melody Maker,* 4/14/79); and various Random Notes, T-zers, Gasbags, Thrills, etc. from *Rolling Stone* (6/2/77, 3/9/78, 5/3/79, 5/18/79, 6/1/78, 6/29/78, 12/14/78; letters 6/28/79, 6/14/79); *NME* (1/8/79, 4/14/79, 4/21/79).

Special thanks to: My editors, Peter, The Golden Disc, Jack and the Bakers; and to Manny, John Nemec and Jeffrey Wong for allowing their record collections to be photographed.